NORSE MYTHOLOGY A TO Z

NORSE MYTHOLOGY A TO Z

A Young Reader's Companion

Kathleen N. Daly

Facts On File, Inc.

NORSE MYTHOLOGY A TO Z

Facts On File, Inc.
11 Penn Plaza
New York NY 10001

Library of Congress Cataloging-in-Publication Data

Daly, Kathleen N.
    Norse mythology A to Z : a young reader's companion / Kathleen N.
Daly.
        p.   cm. — (Mythology A to Z)
    Includes bibliographical references and index.
    Summary: More than 400 alphabetically listed entries identify and
explain the characters, events, and important places of Norse
mythology.
        ISBN 0-8160-2150-3
        1. Mythology, Norse—Dictionaries, Juvenile.   [1. Mythology,
    Norse—Dictionaries.]   I. Title.   II. Series: Daly, Kathleen N.
        Mythology A to Z.
BL850.D34   1991   90-25678
293'.13'03—dc20

Facts On File books are available at special discounts when purchased in
bulk quantities for businesses, associations, institutions, or sales
promotions. Please call our Special Sales Department in New York at
212/967-8800 or 800/322-8755.

Text design by Ron Monteleone
Jacket design by Catherine Hyman

Printed in the United States of America

TSI VB 10 9 8 7 6 5 4 3 2

This book is printed on acid-free paper.

To my own favorite Norse people and their families
(in alphabetical order):
Helen, Jorgen, Kirsten and Ole

CONTENTS

ILLUSTRATION ACKNOWLEDGMENTS

Pages x, xi, 3, 6, 14, 17, 23, 40, 50, 52, 53, 59, 70, 74 (right), 87, 94, 97, 98, New York Public Library Picture Collection; pages 9, 19, 37, 44, Historical Pictures Service–Chicago; pages 12, 25, 26, 28, 49, 51, 66, 74 (left), 75, 77, 82, 91, 96, Anthony Mercatante; page 39, illustration by Johannes Gehrts, Anthony Mercatante collection; page 57, North Wind Picture Archives; page 67, Associated Press-World Wide Photos; page 67, illustration by William Keith, John Wiley & Sons Photo Library; page 68, illustration by Grant M. Haist, National Audubon Society; page 73, Universitetets Oldsaksamling, John Wiley & Sons Book Development Group; page 79, illustration by Sigurdur Thorarinsson, Raunivisindastofnun Haskolans Science Institute, U. of Iceland, John Wiley & Sons Photo Library; page 82, illustration by W. G. Collingwood, Anthony Mercatante.

INTRODUCTION

WHAT IS A MYTH?

There are almost as many definitions of mythology as there are myths. However, everyone seems to agree that myths are as ancient as humankind and have their origin in the efforts of primitive people to explain the mysteries of the world around them: thunder and lightning, floods and fire, rain and drought, earthquakes and volcanic eruptions, night and day, the sun, the moon and the stars, the seasons, the existence of plants and animals, of man and woman, birth and death. Above all, the myths fulfilled a need to believe in some higher being or beings who had power over the daily lives and fate of humankind—a Sky God or All-Father, an Earth Mother and in many cases, such as in the myths of the Norse, a set of attendant gods and goddesses, as well as villains such as demons, dragons and other monsters, giants and dwarfs and supernatural forces.

As well as helping to explain natural phenomena, the myths helped people to structure their lives. The myths reflect their codes of behavior, their cultural customs and rites, such as birth, adolescence, marriage and death, and their ways of worship. In much the same way, religious beliefs help people to live in a way that is both secure and socially acceptable.

Myths are basically stories of the struggle between good and evil, between order and chaos. They foretell of the eventual breakdown of order, but also of regeneration.

The myths about the creation of the universe and the living creatures on earth were passed on orally from one generation to another, from family to family and from one community to another. The stories changed according to the whim of the narrator, for it was thousands of years before the stories were written down. As people migrated, the stories were adapted to the changing landscape or climate. Stories that may have originated in India, the Middle East and the south of Europe changed drastically when they were told in the harsh, craggy, icy lands of the North, where summers were short and winters long and cruel.

While myths express the thoughts of the mysteries of existence, the gods believed in and the social rites of people of one particular time and place, legends are stories that have a semihistorical base. Such legends include the stories of King Arthur in England, Siegfried of the Rhine and Count Dracula in Romania. These heroes or villains really existed, but it's highly unlikely that they performed half the feats that were ascribed to them in legend.

Folktales are stories made up purely for entertainment, though many of them have their base in mythology. For example, the stories about dwarfs and giants that occur in folktales of the North have an obvious connection with the fact that dwarfs and giants feature in Norse mythology.

WHO WERE THE NORSE?

The Norse (people of the North) are known today as the Scandinavians: the people of Norway, Sweden, Denmark, Iceland and the Faroe Islands.

Norsemen are often thought of only as the fierce warriors of the Viking Age (A.D. 780–1070). However, Norse culture originated long before the dramatic explorations of the Vikings. It probably started to take root during the Bronze Age (1600–450 B.C.). No written sources describe early Norse culture, but surviving works in metal and stone depict gods and goddesses and provide glimpses of ancient myths and rituals. The Norse were superb shipbuilders and navigators, intrepid explorers and people with a strong sense of family and clan loyalty. They also loved a good story, a quick wit and fine craftsmanship, which can be seen in the ancient carvings, weaponry and utensils that survive. It is not surprising that the mythology

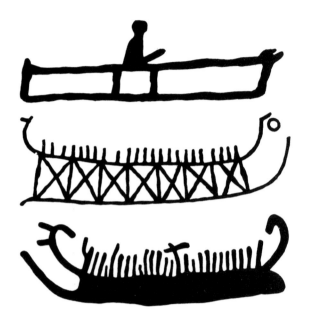

ROCK CARVINGS OF THE EARLIEST NORSE SHIPS, FROM NORWAY AND SWEDEN.

of these strong, lively people was rich, vigorous and witty.

Their mythology originated, it is thought, in Asia, was modified in the European Mediterranean lands and eventually was carried north and west by migrating Teutonic tribes, in the third to sixth centuries A.D. during the breakup of the Roman Empire. The roaming tribes included Angles and Saxons, Goths, Visigoths and Ostrogoths, Allamani, Vandals, Franks and others. As the migrating tribes settled, bringing their myths with them, the old stories began to change with the local geography, climate and temperament of the local people. Later, during the Viking Age, Norsemen began to explore and populate countries from the British Isles and the rest of Europe to Iceland, America, the Near East, Byzantium and Russia, bringing with them their myths and their culture. However, the Norse myths were not written down until the 13th century, by which time Christianity was established in northern Europe and had displaced paganism, that is, the worship and the myths of the ancient gods. Thus much of the ancient lore has been lost forever. What remains is fragmented, incomplete and often distorted by the pious Christian monks who edited the pagan tales as they transcribed them onto parchment for the first time. Although the Norse myths as we know them today are often confusing and contradictory, they still present us with wonderful tales about our vigorous northern ancestors.

THE SOURCES OF THE NORSE MYTHS

The main sources of the Norse myths are the poetry of the early skalds (poets), transmitted orally until the 13th century; The *Poetic Edda*, a sort of anthology of poems written by different poets at different times between the 8th and the 13th centuries; The *Prose Edda*, a handbook for poets and scholars, written by Icelandic poet, scholar, historian and diplomat Snorri Sturluson, around 1220; *Gesta Danorum*, written by the Dane Saxo Grammaticus about 1215; and historical observations by Roman author Tacitus, notably in *Germania* (end of the first century A.D.); Arab traveler Ibn Fadlan (10th century A.D.); Adam of Bremen, 11th century A.D.; *Landnamabok (Book of Settlements)*, 13th century A.D.; and the 13th-century Icelandic sagas (about seven hundred of them), written by authors unknown, which are a valuable source of information about pre-Christian beliefs and practices, kings and bishops, Norse exploration and settlement and legendary heroes such as Sigurd the Volsung.

HOW TO USE THIS BOOK

The entries in this book are in alphabetical order and may be looked up as you would use a dictionary. However, in case you are not familiar with the Norse myths, here is a list of the chief characters and the stories in which they are most important. If you search out the entries concerning these characters, you will get a general overview of Norse mythology. The Index at the back of the book will help you to find the following stories and characters and many more. Cross references to other entries are printed in SMALL CAPITAL letters; names of stories are "in quotes."

First the gods, who numbered twelve, listed roughly in order of their importance in the myths that we know today:

ODIN The one-eyed god, the All-Father, the god of wisdom and poetry, of war and death, plays a principal role in many of the myths, including those of the CREATION, the WAR BE-TWEEN THE AESIR AND THE VANIR, "The Death of Balder" (see under BALDER) and RAGNAROK (the end of the world). Ever in search of wisdom, Odin sacrificed one eye to MIMIR the Wise; in "Lord of the Gallows" (see under ODIN), Odin hanged himself from the World Tree YGGDRA-SIL; he wrested "The Mead of Poetry" from the giant Suttung (see under ODIN); he intoned words of wisdom and lore in the story "Geirrod and Agnar" (see under GEIRROD). In the "Lay of Harbard" he bested his son, THOR, in an exchange of boasts and insults; in "Thor's Duel with Hrungnir" (see under THOR) he defeated the giant Hrungnir in a horse race; and he founded VALHALLA, a mighty hall for slain heroes.

AN ANCIENT DEPICTION OF THOR.

THOR God of thunder, son of ODIN and FRIGGA. He was the strongest of the gods, of fiery temper but well loved. He had a hammer, MJOLLNIR, a magic belt and iron gauntlets and was forever at war with the giants GEIRROD, HYMIR, HRUNGNIR, UTGARD-LOKI, and also the JORMUNGAND, the Midgard Serpent.

BALDER Son of ODIN and FRIGGA. He was the most beautiful and beloved of the gods. There is only one myth about him (see under BALDER), but it is one of the best known of the Norse myths.

NIORD A VANIR god of the seas and seafarers. Niord has two major moments in the myths—as a hostage sent to ASGARD, the home of the AESIR gods, along with the twin deities FREY and FREYA, his children; and as the husband of the giantess SKADE.

FREY A VANIR god, sent to ASGARD as a hostage along with his twin sister FREYA and his father, NIORD. Frey was a god of fertility, peace and plenty, and was much worshiped. In the story "Frey and Gerda," he woos and wins the JOTUN maiden GERDA.

TYR One of the most ancient gods and the most mysterious; he was the bravest and most just of the gods when he undertook to put his hand into the jaws of the terrible wolf, FENRIS.

BRAGI Called the god of poetry, he was a minor figure in the surviving myths; married to IDUNN and possibly the son of ODIN and GUN-LOD, the JOTUN maiden from whom Odin stole "The Mead of Poetry" (see under ODIN).

HEIMDALL The watchman of the gods who guarded BIFROST, the Rainbow Bridge that connected ASGARD, the domain of the gods, with MIDGARD, the Middle Earth. Heimdall had a trumpet, GJALLAR, with which he would summon the gods to battle at RAGNAROK. In one myth ("Rig-Heimdall and the Races of Men," see under HEIMDALL) he goes down to earth and fathers the classes of men and women into which society was divided in the Viking world.

VIDAR Son of ODIN who will avenge his father's death at RAGNAROK by slaying FENRIS, the wolf.

VALI ODIN's youngest son who will avenge BALDER's death by slaying HODUR.

ULL The stepson of THOR and SIF. Not much is known about him, except that he was a god of snow, skiers and archery. His name survives in many Scandinavian and British place names, so he must have been more important in bygone days.

FORSETI Son of BALDER and NANNA. Nothing much is known about him, except that he had to do with justice and fairness.

And then there is LOKI:

LOKI A god or a demon or a mixture of both, the mischievous Loki is involved in many of the myths, including "Asgard's Wall and the Giant Builder" (see under ASGARD), "The Theft of Thor's Hammer" (see under THOR), THE TREASURES OF THE DWARFS; Loki accompanies THOR on encounters with the giants HYMIR and UTGARD-LOKI; he arranged BALDER's death; insulted all the gods and goddesses at Aegir's banquet (see "Loki's Mocking," under LOKI); stole the necklace of the goddess Freya (see "Freya's Golden Necklace," under FREYA); stole Sif's golden hair (see THE TREASURES OF THE DWARFS); was chained to a rock by the gods in "The Punishment of Loki" (see under LOKI); and helped to lead the forces of evil against the gods at RAGNAROK.

The goddesses play a minor role in the surviving Norse myths.

FRIGGA The wife of ODIN. Her greatest role is in the myth of BALDER, her beloved son, whom she tries to protect from death.

FREYA The goddess of fertility, the sister of FREY, the daughter of NIORD. She is beautiful and has a fatal love of gold (see "Freya's Golden Necklace," under FREYA); she is loved by DWARFS and giants alike; perhaps acquainted with magic and prophecy; but few facts are known about her, and she is often confused with FRIGGA.

IDUNN The keeper of the apples of youth, she is heard of only in the myth "Idunn and the Golden Apples" (see under IDUNN).

Other females in the Norse myths are the NORNS and the VALKYRIE. The Norns are the three Fates who represent the Past, the Present and the Future, and who determine the destiny of all living creatures. The Norns are more powerful even than the gods.

The Valkyrie are Odin's warrior maidens who select the fallen heroes and carry them to Odin's hall, VALHALLA.

The forces of evil are represented chiefly by the offspring of LOKI: HEL, queen of death and the underworld; FENRIS, the monster wolf; and JORMUNGAND, the Midgard Serpent who is so huge that he encircles the earth and holds his tail in his mouth. Other wolves chase after the sun and the moon and numerous JOTUN try to outwit and outfight the gods.

A

AEGIR The JOTUN lord of the sea. He was married to his sister, RAN, and was the father of nine daughters, the waves, who were said to be the mothers of the god HEIMDALL. Some stories say that Aegir was the brother of LOKI and Kari (Air). He belonged to a primeval order of gods, predating both the AESIR and the VANIR, and the giants, DWARFS and ELVES. Aegir is usually pictured as an old man with long white hair and clawlike hands. His dwelling is on the island of HLESEY, in coral caves beneath the land. His servants are ELDIR and FIMAFENG. (See "Loki's Mocking," under LOKI, which takes place at a banquet in Aegir's hall; "Otter's Ransom," under OTTER, in which Loki borrows RAN's fishing net; and "Thor and Hymir Go Fishing," under THOR, in which THOR and TYR bring back a cauldron that Aegir uses to brew ale for the feasting of the gods.)

In Anglo-Saxon mythology Aegir was called Eagor. Whenever an unusually large wave approached men at sea, they cried, "Look out, Eagor is coming!" Supposedly, in ancient Saxon times one out of every 10 prisoners was sacrificed to Eagor to ensure that the raiders would return safely home.

AESIR The race of gods who lived in ASGARD under the leadership of the chief god, ODIN. Other gods included, in alphabetical order, BALDER, the beautiful; BRAGI, god of poetry; FORSETI, god of justice; FREY, god of fertility; HEIMDALL, the watchman of the gods; NIORD, the sea god; THOR, god of thunder; TYR, a brave sky god; ULL, a winter god; VALI, the avenger; and VIDAR, the silent god.

Not many myths survive about the goddesses except for those concerning FREYA, fertility goddess; FRIGGA, wife of Odin; IDUNN, keeper of the apples of youth; and SIF, the golden-haired wife of Thor.

AGNAR Son of King Hrauding, brother of GEIRROD. When he and his brother were shipwrecked, they were befriended by an old couple who were ODIN and FRIGGA in disguise. Frigga took special care of Agnar, who was eventually betrayed by his brother, Odin's protegé. (See "Geirrod and Agnar," under GEIRROD.) In later years another Agnar (probably the son of Geirrod) took pity on Odin, who had been captured and slung between two fires. After Agnar had given Odin ale to quench his thirst, Odin chanted a song that was known as "Grimnirsmal" or "The Lay of Grimnir."

ALBERICH The dwarf in Richard Wagner's 19th-century opera cycle, THE RING OF THE NIBELUNG. In the myth "Otter's Ransom" (see under OTTER), Alberich (the king of the elves) is called ANDVARI.

ALFRIGG One of the four DWARFS who made the Brising necklace for the goddess Freya. The others were Berling, Dvalin and Grerr. (See "Freya and the Golden Necklace" under FREYA.)

ALL-FATHER Another name for the god ODIN.

ALL-SWIFT (Alsvid) One of the two horses that draws the sun's chariot driven by the fair maiden SOL. (See "Sun and Moon," under CREATION.) The other horse is EARLY WAKER (ARVAKR).

ALSVID (All-Swift) One of the two horses that draws the sun's chariot driven by the fair maiden SOL. The other horse is ARVAKR (EARLY WAKER). (See "Sun and Moon," under CREATION.)

ALSVIDER (Rapid Goer) The horse that pulled the moon's chariot for MANI. (See "Sun and Moon," under CREATION.)

ALVIS (All Wise) A DWARF who was turned to stone. He had come to ASGARD to claim the bride (THRUD, daughter of the god THOR) the gods had promised him. Thor, knowing that Alvis, like many dwarfs, liked to show off his considerable knowledge, lured him into a lengthy question-and-answer game. He asked Alvis for alternative names for the 13 words that were most important in the lives of medieval Scandinavians. (See "Words of Alvis," below.) Alvis talked as the night wore on. At the end the sun, which the dwarf had called "DVALIN'S DELIGHT," came up and turned Alvis to stone, which was the fate of the dwarf Dvalin and of all dwarfs caught in the sunlight.

WORDS OF ALVIS

WORDS	MEN	GODS	GIANTS	DWARFS AND ELVES
EARTH	earth	fields, ways	evergreen place	growing place, clay
HEAVEN	heaven	warmer of the heights	wind weaver	high home, fair roof, dripping hall
MOON	moon	mock sun	night traveler	month teller, gleamer, whirling wheel
SUN	sun, sol	shining orb	ever bright	fair wheel, Dvalin's delight
CLOUDS	sky, skies	shower bringers	wind floes, wind kites	rain bearers, weather tellers, helmets of darkness
WIND	wind	waverer, noise maker	whooper, wailer	roaring traveler, blusterer

WORDS OF ALVIS

WORDS	MEN	GODS	GIANTS	DWARFS AND ELVES
CALM	calm	quietness	wind's husk	sultry, day's lull, day's refuge
MAIN	sea	home of waves	home of eels	the big drink, the deep
FIRE	fire	flamer	greedy one	furnace, burner, destroyer
WOOD	wood	shelter of the fields	fuel	fair limbs, adorner of the hills
NIGHT	night	darkness	day's mask	unlight, soother, bringer of dreams
SEED	barley	grain, grower	food maker	slender stalk maker
ALE	ale	beer, foamer	swill	good cheer, mead

These words are taken from "The Lay of Alvis" ("Alvismal") in the *Edda*.

AMSVARTNIR The lake in which stood the island of LYNGVI, where the gods bound the wolf FENRIS.

ANDHRIMNIR (Sooty Faced) VALHALLA's cook, whose job it was to cook the magic boar, SAEHRIMNIR, each night for the feasting of the gods and heroes.

ANDVARANAUT (Andvari's Loom) The magic ring stolen from the dwarf ANDVARI by LOKI. The ring worked like a magnet to attract gold. (See "Otter's Ransom," under OTTER.)

ANDVARI A DWARF who is robbed of his hoard of gold by LOKI, the trickster god. Andvari has put a curse upon a ring, which is called ANDVARANAUT, part of the treasure. The treasure is given to the magician REIDMAR in compensation for the killing of his son, OTTER, by Loki. (See "Otter's Ransom," under OTTER.) In Richard Wagner's 19th-century opera cycle THE RING OF THE NIBELUNG, Andvari is called Alberich.

ANGERBODA, AURBODA (Bringer of Distress) The ogress wife of LOKI and mother of the wolf FENRIS, HEL, goddess of death, and JORMUN-GAND, the Midgard Serpent.

In some tellings she was also the mother of GERDA (who married the god FREY) and the wife of the giant GYMIR.

ANNAR (Another) The second husband of NIGHT. Their daughter was EARTH. (See "Night and Day," under CREATION.)

APPLE The apple tree is a fruit tree common throughout the temperate regions of the world.

IN GENESIS, IN THE OLD TESTAMENT, ADAM AND EVE EAT THE FORBIDDEN FRUIT OF THE APPLE TREE.

It is used as a symbol of love, fertility and youth in many mythologies, including the Norse (see "Idunn's Apples," under IDUNN) and Greek (Paris and Aphrodite). In the Old Testament (Genesis 2:4–4:26) the apple is a symbol of evil knowledge. However, many scholars believe that the fruit intended was not an apple but a pomegranate and that early translators of the Gospels made a deliberate pun from the word *malum*, which in Latin means both "apple" and "evil."

ARVAKR (Early Waker) One of the two horses that draws the sun's chariot across the sky for the fair maiden SOL. (See "Sun and Moon," under CREATION.) The other horse is ALSVID (All-Swift).

ASGARD The realm of the AESIR gods, presided over by ODIN. It was the topmost level of the NINE WORLDS. Here the gods and goddesses had their palaces and mansions, called halls. Asgard was surrounded and protected by a mighty wall built by a giant. (See "Asgard's Wall and the Giant Builder," below.) In the center of Asgard was the green field, IDAVOLD, around which stood the 13 halls of the gods; among them were GLADSHEIM, the main hall of the gods; BILSKIRNIR, the hall of THOR; FENSALIR, which belonged to FRIGGA; BREIDABLIK, where BALDER and his wife, NANNA, lived; HIMINBJORG, the abode of HEIMDALL; GLITNIR, where FORSETI presided; SESSRUMNIR, FREYA'S hall; and VALHALLA, where Odin entertained the slain heroes of the world. Asgard was connected to MIDGARD (Middle Earth) by the Rainbow Bridge, BIFROST. At RAGNAROK, the end of the world, all the beautiful mansions would be destroyed. But the golden playthings of the gods, chess pieces, would remain, and a new world would arise. (See "The Regeneration," under RAGNAROK.)

Asgard's Wall and the Giant Builder The AESIR gods wanted to build a new wall around their stronghold, ASGARD. The VANIR had destroyed the original wall in the first and last battle between the two races of gods. (See THE WAR BETWEEN THE AESIR AND THE VANIR.)

The gods were good at building fine halls and glittering palaces, but to build a fortresslike wall seemed an enormous task.

One day a large man trotted his horse over BIFROST, the Rainbow Bridge, and told HEIMDALL, the watchman god, that he had a plan to put before the gods. Heimdall reported the news to the chief god, ODIN, who assembled all the gods and goddesses together to meet the stranger.

The tall man, who was the giant HRIMTHURS in disguise, said that he would rebuild the wall around Asgard in 18 months. For his fee, he would take the goddess FREYA to be his wife. He would also take the sun and the moon.

The gods roared with anger. Odin said angrily that he would never part with beautiful Freya, nor with the sun and the moon, which gave warmth and light to the world. He bade the mason leave.

But LOKI, the sly god, begged the gods not to be hasty. He asked the mason for some time to consider his plan. The mason left the hall and the gods and goddesses clustered around Loki, while Freya began to weep tears of gold.

Loki suggested that if they could get the mason to promise to build the wall in six months' time—before spring came—they would have nothing to fear, for obviously it was impossible for anyone to complete the wall so quickly. But at least the mason could dig the foundation and get a good start on the wall, thus saving the gods a lot of work. And, said Loki, they wouldn't have to pay him a thing.

Odin called the builder back into the hall and told him their decision. At first the mason seemed dismayed by how little time he would have to finish the work. But at last he agreed to try, provided that he could have his great stallion, SVADILFARI, to help him. The bargain was struck.

As he began to build the wall, the gods looked on in amazement. Never had they seen a man cut such huge blocks of stone, nor a horse pull such heavy loads. The wall began to take shape, getting higher and higher and stronger and stronger. Though the winter was cruel, the tall man labored on undaunted.

At last the cold and the snow and the ice

abated. The last day of winter was near and the wall was almost finished.

The gods met again. If the mason finished the wall in time, they would lose their treasured Freya and the sun and the moon. Suddenly they wondered how they had arrived at this terrible predicament. Then they remembered. They threw dark looks at Loki.

Odin sternly told Loki to use his cunning once again, this time to save the goddess Freya and the sun and the moon. Terrified at Odin's anger, Loki promised that he would find a way to outwit the builder.

That evening, as the mason led Svadilfari toward the pile of stones to be hauled, the stallion pranced gaily. He could smell spring in the air. Suddenly he spied a beautiful young mare. She danced up to him and swished her tail. It was more than Svadilfari could stand. With a mighty bound he broke free of his harness and bolted after the mare.

The mason shouted with rage and set off in pursuit, but it was useless. Svadilfari had had a long, lonely winter, and now he wanted some lighthearted fun with the pretty mare.

Dawn came, and with it the end of winter.

The wall was incomplete. The mason lost the bargain and was slain by the thunder god, THOR, who had returned from his travels.

When Loki came back to Asgard several months later, he was leading a handsome young colt. It had eight legs and obviously would grow up to be a magnificent horse. Indeed, its father was the mighty Svadilfari, and its mother was none other than Loki himself, who had disguised himself as the pretty mare.

Odin claimed the colt for his own and named it SLEIPNIR, the glider.

This is the first myth that shows up the enmity between the gods and the giants—a theme that occurs in most of the myths and doesn't end until RAGNAROK. When the giant demands the sun and the moon and also Freya, he intends to deprive the gods not only of the four seasons but also of the possibility of regeneration, for Freya was the goddess of love and fertility. This is also the first myth in which Loki plays the part of mischief maker and shape-changer. He gets the gods into trouble;

but he also gets them out of it by changing himself into a mare.

The only complete version of this myth is in SNORRI STURLUSON'S PROSE EDDA.

ASH A tree of the olive family (genus *Fraxinus*). In Norse mythology the sacred ash, or World Tree, YGGDRASIL, plays a dominant part in the makeup of the NINE WORLDS.

The first man was created when the AESIR gods breathed life into the trunk of an ash tree. (See "The First Humans," under CREATION.)

ASH, MOUNTAIN See ROWAN.

ASK The first man, created from the trunk of an ASH tree by the first three AESIR gods, ODIN, VILI and VE. (See "The First Humans," under CREATION.) All human beings, it is said in Norse mythology, are descended from Ask and EMBLA, the first woman.

ASYNJER, ASYNJUR The goddesses of the AESIR, led by FRIGG.

AUD The son of NIGHT and her first husband, NAGLFARI.

AUDHUMLA The first cow, formed at the creation of the world. She appeared at the same time as YMIR, the first giant, and fed him with her milk. She herself derived nourishment by licking the salty stones around GINNUNGAGAP, the primeval abyss. As she licked, she uncovered a handsome, manlike creature from the ice. He was BURI, the first ancestor of the gods. (See CREATION.)

In many mythologies the cow is a symbol of the Great Mother and of creation. Audhumla appears in the PROSE EDDA and in the POETIC EDDA.

AURBODA The mother of the giantess GERDA, beloved of the god FREY. (See "Frey and Gerda," under FREY.) Aurboda was possibly another name for ANGERBODA, the wife of LOKI.

AURORA BOREALIS Shimmering lights or luminescence that sometimes appear in night

IN NORSE MYTHOLOGY THE AURORA BOREALIS OR NORTHERN LIGHTS ARE THE PERSONIFICATION OF GERDA.

skies in the Northern Hemisphere. Also called Northern Lights. In Norse mythology this beautiful sight was said to be the radiance emitted from GERDA, the JOTUN maiden who became the wife of the god Frey. (See "Frey and Gerda," under FREY.)

AURVANDIL Known as The Brave, he was the husband of the seeress GROA. Not much is known about him except that the god THOR rescues him from the giants and carries him across the poisonous rivers of ELIVAGAR in a basket. One of Aurvandil's toes freezes. Thor plucks it off and throws it into the sky, where it shines forevermore as a bright star known as Aurvandil's Toe. (We do not know today which star it is.) (See "Thor's Duel with Hrungnir," under THOR.)

AUSTRI (East) One of the four DWARFS who held up the SKY. (See CREATION.)

B

BALDER Balder was the beloved son of the great god ODIN and of his wife FRIGGA. The story of the god Balder is one of the most famous and one of the most complete in Norse mythology. It has been retold many times over the centuries, from SNORRI STURLUSON's account in the PROSE EDDA, to the story of the Danish scholar SAXO GRAMMATICUS, to the poem by the English poet Matthew Arnold ("Balder Dead"). Many scholars think that the portrayal of the beautiful, good, passive god Balder was influenced by early Christian views of Jesus Christ.

Balder's Dreams When Balder became a young man, he began to have fearful dreams that seemed to foretell his death. Not one of the gods could understand the meaning of these dreams. His unhappiness cast a pall upon all who lived in ASGARD, the home of the gods.

Odin's Visit to the Vala Odin, determined to solve the mystery of his son's dreams, mounted his horse, SLEIPNIR, and made the long journey to the underworld, NIFLHEIM. There he called up a seeress, one of the VALA. When she arose from her tomb, Odin introduced himself as VEGTAM, the Wanderer, son of Valtam.

Odin asked the Vala why the halls of HEL were decked with gold and the tables set for a grisly feast. The seeress replied that it was for Balder.

Odin asked who would slay Balder. The seeress answered that the blind HODUR would cast a fatal branch at his brother.

Odin asked who would avenge Balder's death. The seeress answered that Odin would take RINDA to wife and their son would be VALI who would take vengeance when he was only one night old. (See "Vali, the Avenger," under VALI.)

Odin asked who would refuse to weep for Balder. At this question, which revealed that "Vegtam" knew or guessed more of the future than

an ordinary mortal could, the Vala realized that Vegtam was in fact Odin, the magician, the All-Father, older than time.

She refused to answer any more questions and sank back into her tomb, vowing to speak no more until LOKI's chains would be unbound— that is, until the end of the world. Because the Vala professed to be the mother of three monsters, she was thought to be Loki, the trickster, in disguise.

Frigga and the Mistletoe When Frigga realized that her son Balder's life was in danger, she sent her messengers to every corner of the world to extract promises not to harm her beloved son. Stones and metals, water and wind, fish and birds, reptiles and mammals, trees and flowers, insects and spiders and scorpions, all creatures alive, all objects large and small, swore that they wouldn't harm Balder. Only one small green plant, the MISTLETOE, which grew on the mighty OAK tree, wasn't asked to make the promise, for it was so frail that nobody paid any attention to it.

The Gods at Play Word soon get around Asgard that Balder was absolutely invulnerable: Nothing could harm him. The young gods, always ready for fun, made a game out of throwing things at Balder: stones, knives, sticks. Whatever they threw glanced off Balder's body, leaving him totally unharmed, to the merriment of all.

Only Loki didn't join in the fun. Instead he disguised himself as an old crone and paid a visit to Frigga. Pretending to be astonished and disgusted at the sport the gods were making of Balder, Loki cunningly got from Frigga the information he sought: that there was indeed one object in the world that had not taken the vow to be harmless to Balder. That object was the mistletoe that grew in the branches of the oak tree outside VALHALLA.

Loki sped off, plucked a sprig of mistletoe and

hastened to the field of IDAVOLL, where the merry young gods were still at play. Only the blind god, Hodur, hung back, for he could not see.

Loki approached Hodur, put the mistletoe branch into his hands and offered to guide his aim; Hodur gladly accepted.

The Death of Balder And so it was that Hodur, Balder's brother, threw the fatal weapon and killed Balder.

When Balder fell dead a terrible silence fell upon the gods, and then began a fearful wailing. Balder, the good, the beautiful, the god of light, had been snuffed out like a bright candle.

The gods would willingly have killed Hodur there and then, but ancient laws forbade that blood should be shed in Idavold, so Hodur slunk off, alone and weeping.

Balder's Funeral Pyre The gods built a huge funeral pyre on RINGHORN, Balder's dragon ship. On it they laid the body, surrounding it with rich tapestries, heaps of flowers, vessels of food, clothes, weapons and precious jewels, as was the custom of the Norse.

Nanna, Balder's loving wife, fell grief-stricken over the body and died, so the gods placed her tenderly on the pyre beside her husband. Then they slew Balder's horse and hounds and placed them beside their master, so that he should lack for nothing.

One by one all the gods drew near to say farewell to their beloved companion. Last of all came Odin, who took off his magic arm ring, and placed it on his son's body. Then he stooped and put his mouth to Balder's ear, but nobody knew what he whispered.

When the gods tried to launch the ship, it was so heavy that not even THOR's phenomenal strength could move it. And so the gods accepted the help of HYROKKIN, a giantess who galloped onto the scene riding a huge wolf and holding reins of writhing snakes. Hyrokkin gave the vessel a mighty shove and launched it into the sea.

The funeral pyre was lighted and Thor went on board to consecrate the fire with his magic hammer, MJOLLNIR. As he was performing the rite, the dwarf LIT got under his feet, and Thor kicked him into the flames, where he burned to

ashes along with Balder and Nanna.

The ship drifted out to sea, burning brightly, and the gods watched it in mourning until it disappeared and the world became dark.

Hermod's Journey When she had recovered sufficiently to speak, Frigga asked that one of the gods go to visit HEL in Niflheim and beg her to send Balder back from the land of the dead. Gallant HERMOD, another of Odin's sons, immediately volunteered to make the dreaded journey. Odin lent him his horse, Sleipnir, and for the second time the brave horse made the journey to the underworld. After traveling for nine days and nine nights and crossing many rivers, Hermod came to a stream, GJALL. Sleipnir's hooves made the bridge over Gjall's stream shudder, and his rider was challenged by the sentry, MODGUD. Upon learning that Balder was indeed in Niflheim, Hermod and Sleipnir made a great leap over the gate of Hel and landed safely on the other side. But Balder could not leave the land of the dead without Hel's permission, and Hel, the churlish, refused to let him go unless all the world should rain tears for him. Hermod spent many hours with Balder and his wife, NANNA. They gave him gifts, including Odin's magic arm ring, DRAUPNIR, to bring back to Asgard.

Then Hermod took his leave and set off to tell the gods his news. Surely the whole world would willingly weep to set Balder free.

Thokk When Hermod returned from the underworld with the news about Hel's condition for the return of Balder, messengers at once set out for every corner of the earth.

Soon every god and goddess, every man and woman, every plant and every animal on land and sea and air, and every stone and metal was shedding tears for Balder.

But in a dark cave sat an old woman, the giantess THOKK. She alone remained dry-eyed and hard of heart. "Balder never did anything for me," she said grimly. "Let Hel keep what is her due, for I have no tears for Balder."

Then the messengers returned to Odin and Frigga with heavy hearts, and the gods mourned once more, for they knew now that Balder would never return to them.

BALDER, THE SHINING GOD, IS SLAIN BY HODUR, WITH THE HELP OF LOKI AND A SPRIG OF MISTLETOE.

Vali Kills Hodur Balder's death was avenged by the death of his unwitting killer, Hodur. Vali, Odin's youngest son, appeared in Asgard on the day of his birth, miraculously grown to full stature and carrying a quiver of arrows. He shot one of these at Hodur, who died. Thus the Norsemen's code of a death for a death was satisfied, and the Vala's prophecy was fulfilled. (See "Vali, The Avenger," under VALI.)

Ragnarok At the REGENERATION (see under RAGNAROK), Balder came back from the dead, leading his blind brother, Hodur. All the survivors of Ragnarok went back to IDAVOLL, where they created a new world.

BARLEY One of the oldest of cultivated cereal grasses, barley is widely distributed throughout the world. There are carvings of it on Egyptian tombs, and it is mentioned in the Bible. In northern lands it was used to make a malt brew and was a symbol of spring growth. In the story "Frey and Gerda" (see under FREY), the barley patch, BARRI, is where Frey and Gerda are united.

BARLEY BYGGVIR One of the god FREY's servants. Married to BEYLA. The couple served at the feast that AEGIR gave to the gods. (See "Loki's Mocking," under LOKI.)

BARRI (Barre) The sacred grove where the god FREY and the JOTUN maid GERDA were united in the story "Frey and Gerda," (see under FREY.) The word derives from BARLEY.

BAUGI A giant, the brother of SUTTUNG. Baugi employs ODIN, who is disguised as a worker, BOLVERK. Bolverk works so well that Baugi agrees to lead him to the mountain where "The Mead of Poetry" (see under ODIN) is hidden, guarded by GUNLOD, Suttung's daughter. Baugi drills a hole in the mountain with his augur, and Odin changes into a serpent and slithers through the hole to find Gunlod and the mead.

BELI The JOTUN brother of GERDA, FREY's beloved. Beli challenged Frey and Frey killed him with a stag horn, as he had given away his magic sword as BRIDE PRICE to GYMIR, Gerda's father. (See "Frey and Gerda," under FREY.)

BERGELMIR Son of the FROST GIANT Thrudgelmir; grandson of YMIR, the primeval giant who appeared at the CREATION. Bergelmir and his wife were the only surviving giants after Ymir's death and the flood. They rode the flood on a hollowed-out tree trunk, the first boat. Because of them, the race of frost giants and ogres was able to survive in JOTUNHEIM. *(Prose Edda.)*

BERLING One of the four dwarfs who made the BRISINGS' NECKLACE for the goddess FREYA. The others were ALFRIGG, DVALIN, and GRERR. (See "Freya and the Golden Necklace," under FREYA.)

BERSERKERS Savage, reckless warriors, an elite corps who fought for ODIN wearing only bear or wolf skins and no armor. In the sagas they were named after Berserk, a Norse hero of the 8th century who went into battle with his 12 sons.

To "run berserk" is to go into a frenzy.

BESTLA The giantess wife of BOR and mother of three gods, ODIN, VILI and VE. She was the daughter of the giant BOLTHUR. Bestla appears in the PROSE EDDA.

BEYLA The wife of BARLEY BYGGVIR. Both were servants of the god FREY who attended a feast given by AEGIR. (See "Loki's Mocking," under LOKI.)

BIFROST (Trembling Path) The flaming, three-strand bridge between ASGARD and MIDGARD, also called the Rainbow Bridge. It is seen by people on earth as a rainbow spanning the distance between heaven and earth.

The AESIR gods skillfully built Bifrost out of fire, air and water, the three materials that can be seen as the colors of the rainbow: red (fire), blue (air) and green (water). Though it looked fragile, Bifrost was immensely strong.

The gods appointed HEIMDALL to be the watchman of the bridge, for his senses were keen and he had a marvelous horn, GIALLAR, whose blast would be heard in all NINE WORLDS if the FROST GIANTS set foot on Bifrost.

The Aesir gods crossed Bifrost regularly to go to council meetings at the Well of URD, a sacred place. Only THOR, the thunder god, could not walk or ride across Bifrost, lest the heat of his lightning and thunderbolts should harm the bridge.

At RAGNAROK, the end of the world, Bifrost would shatter under the terrible weight of the sons of MUSPELLHEIM, the frost giants who came to fight the gods on VIGRID, the vast battlefield.

BIL AND YUKI (or HJUKI) (the Waxing and Waning moon) The two earth children stolen by MANI, the man of the moon, to help him drive his chariot across the skies. They were the children of VIDFINN. They had been sent by him to fetch water from the spring BYRGIR in a pail (SOEG) carried between them on a pole (SIMUL). Legend has it that the shadows we see on the moon are those of the two children carrying their pail of water. (See "Sun and Moon," under CREATION.)

A 19th-century Englishman, the Reverend S. Baring-Gould, in *Curious Myths of the Middle Ages* (1866) claimed that the popular nursery rhyme about "Jack and Jill," who "went up the hill to fetch a pail of water" had its origin in the ancient tale of Bil and Yuki.

BILLING, KING In some tellings of the myths King Billing is king of the Ruthenians (Russians) and the father of RINDA, who was to be wooed by ODIN. (See "Vali, The Avenger," under VALI.)

BILSKIRNIR (Lightning) THOR's dwelling in ASGARD. As befitted the god's large size and his fondness for giving huge banquets, Bilskirnir, with 540 rooms, was the largest hall in all Asgard.

BLODIGHOFI See BLOODYHOOF.

BLOODYHOOF The god FREY's magical horse that could leap through flames unharmed. Also called BLODIGHOFI. (See "Frey and Gerda," under FREY.)

BOAR A male swine or pig. It has been admired since ancient times for its courage; it has been hunted and killed for its succulent flesh, tough bristles, sturdy hide, sharp tusks—in fact, no part of this creature goes unused by humankind.

In Norse mythology and history FREY's golden boar was named GULLINBURSTI (Golden Bristles). Gullinbursti's image is found on many helmets and shields worn by ancient warriors as a symbol of good luck in battle. In the winter months a sacrificial boar was offered up to the god Frey. The pagan custom is still remembered in many countries at Yuletide or Christmas, where roast pig, pork or ham may be the festive dish. In Sweden Yuletide cakes are baked in the shape of a boar. In England many inns are called The Boar's Head in recognition of the ancient custom of serving a boar's head at Christmas.

Also mentioned in Norse mythology is the golden boar, HILDISVINI, belonging to Frey's sister, FREYA, and the boar SAEHRIMNIR, who was nightly sacrificed at ODIN's VALHALLA for the feasting of the heroes. Saehrimnir came back to life again every day.

BODN (Vessel) One of the jars in which the blood of KVASIR was kept. (See "The Mead of Poetry," under ODIN.)

BOLTHUR also BOLTHORN, BOLTURON (Thorn of Evil) The jotun father of BESTLA and of a son whose name is unknown. Bestla married BOR and bore him three sons, ODIN, VILI and VE. Thus Bolthur was Odin's grandfather.

When Odin hanged himself from the World Tree, YGGDRASIL, to gain wisdom, he learned nine songs from the son of Bolthor, who was his uncle. In Norse mythology and folklore there was often a close bond between a man and his maternal uncle, who sometimes acted as godfather or guardian or surrogate father. (See "Lord of the Gallows," under ODIN.)

BOLVERK (Evil-Doer) The name assumed by ODIN when he went to JOTUNHEIM to steal back "The Mead of Poetry" (see under ODIN). He took the form of a tall, strong man. When he found nine slaves working wearily in a field, he offered to sharpen their scythes with his whetstone. The slaves were so impressed with the sharpness of their blades after Bolverk had honed them that they asked for the whetstone. Odin-Bolverk threw it up in the air; as they scrambled to catch it, the nine workers managed to kill each other with their scythes. Thus Odin-Bolverk was able to ingratiate himself with their master, BAUGI, who now had no workers, and was glad to employ the stranger. As a reward for his work, Baugi eventually led Odin to the cave where the Mead of Poetry was hidden.

The character of Bolverk shows Odin as a devious, cruel being who will shed the blood of others to gain his ends.

BOR An early god, the son of BURI and the husband of the giantess BESTLA. Bor and Bestla had three sons, the gods ODIN, VILI and VE.

BRAGI The god of poetry, eloquence and music. Son of ODIN and GUNLOD, husband of IDUNN. Bragi does not play a major role in Norse myths, but it is clear that he is revered by all except LOKI (see "Loki's Mocking," under LOKI.) He is pictured as playing on a harp and singing so sweetly that even the trees and flowers are charmed by him. Norsemen called their poets or skalds *bragamen* or *bragawomen*. In English the verb "to brag" means "to boast rather loudly of one's achievements."

Because Odin had a great knowledge of poetry (see "The Mead of Poetry," under ODIN), some scholars see Bragi as another facet of Odin's personality.

BREIDABLIK (Broad Gleaming) The shining hall of the god BALDER in ASGARD.

BRIDE (or BRIDAL) PRICE In ancient times, and still among some primitive people, the money or goods given to the family of the bride by the bridegroom or his family. In the story "Frey and Gerda" (see under FREY), Frey's magic sword was the bride price for Gerda. In another Norse story the giant THRYM offers THOR's stolen hammer in return for FREYA as his bride. (See "The Theft of Thor's Hammer," under THOR.)

BRISINGAMEN See BRISINGS' NECKLACE.

BRISINGS' NECKLACE or BRISINGAMEN
The golden necklace given to the goddess FREYA by the four DWARFS, ALFRIGG, BERLING, DVALIN and GRERR. It is not known who the Brisings were. Freya was the goddess of fertility; a necklace is often used as a fertility symbol. (See "Freya and the Golden Necklace," under FREYA.)

Freya lends the necklace to the god THOR in "The Theft of Thor's Hammer" (see under THOR).

BROKK a DWARF, brother of SINDRI. Together the two brothers crafted fabulous treasures. (See THE TREASURES OF THE DWARFS.)

BRUNHILDA (Warrior in Armor) A VALKYRIE (warrior maiden), daughter of ODIN. In the VOL-SUNGA SAGA she is the leader of the Valkyries. She disobeys Odin, who punishes her by putting her to sleep and surrounding her resting place with a ring of fire. Brunhilda falls in love with the hero SIGURD when he rescues her. Sigurd gives her a magic ring but then abandons her for Gutrune. In the end Sigurd is killed and placed upon a funeral pyre. Brunhilda, who has caused his death, is stricken with remorse and throws herself (and the ring) into the fire. This story appears in Richard Wagner's 19th-century music-drama, THE RING OF THE NIBELUNG.

BRUNHILDA, THE VALKYRIE MAIDEN, SURROUNDED BY FIRE.

BURI Ancestor of the gods. He appeared at the time of the CREATION, when the cosmic cow, AUDHUMLA, brought him to life from under the primeval ice. In time Buri had a son called BOR, who married the giantess BESTLA and became the father of the gods ODIN, VILI and VE.

BYRGIR The well to which the earth children, BIL AND YUKI had gone to fetch water before being stolen away by MANI, the man of the moon. (See "Sun and Moon," under CREATION.)

C

CAT General name for the feline species. In world mythology the domestic cat is often venerated (as in Egypt) or feared as a witch in disguise or as a witch's "creature." In Norse mythology the goddess FREYA, who had magic powers, had a chariot drawn by two gray or black cats.

CAULDRON A large pot or kettle used for boiling. In "Thor and Hymir Go Fishing," (see under THOR), Thor goes in search of Hymir's huge cauldron because the gods need it for brewing ale; later, in "Loki's Mocking," (see under LOKI), the sea god AEGIR gives a banquet for the gods. He brews the ale in the cauldron that Thor and Tyr took from Hymir. The cauldron features in many medieval tales, especially those where witches brew magic broths. The three witches in Shakespeare's *Macbeth* brew their potion in a cauldron.

COW A female mammal, noted for the nurturing properties of her milk. In many world mythologies she is the symbol of the Great Mother and of Creation. In the PROSE EDDA and the POETIC EDDA of the Norse, the cow is AUDHUMLA. (See CREATION.)

CREATION The mythology of each people has its own story of how the world was created. Perhaps the best known in our culture is the story told in Genesis, the first book of the Old Testament of the Judeo-Christian religion. In Norse mythology, at the beginning there was a swirling chaos of mists and fog, freezing cold, howling winds and terrifying fire.

There was no sun; no moon; no stars; no land or sea; there was only a yawning chasm called GINNUNGAGAP.

To the north of Ginnungagap was NIFLHEIM, land of cold mists; to the south was MUSPELLHEIM, the land of fire. From Niflheim's spring, HVERGELMIR, flowed the 11 poisonous rivers of the ELIVAGAR. They emptied into the chasm and froze and filled it with venomous ice. From Muspellheim came sheets of fire that turned the ice into mists and dense fog.

For millions of years fire and ice interacted with each other until at last there came sparks of life. The first life took the form of a huge, ugly giant, YMIR, and a gigantic cow, AUDHUMLA.

Audhumla nourished Ymir with her milk, and she in turn licked the salty stones around Ginnungagap for nourishment.

As Audhumla continued to lick away at the icy, salty stones around Ginnungagap, she uncovered the hairs of a man's head. Soon she uncovered the entire head and finally, the whole body of a handsome, manlike creature. He was BURI, the ancestor of the gods.

Buri produced a son named BOR, who married a giantess, BESTLA, who gave him three sons, ODIN, VILI and VE, the first gods.

Meanwhile, as Ymir slept on, hordes of hideous giant children sprouted from his body. They were the FROST GIANTS, or JOTUNS.

Odin and his brothers, the sons of Bor, quarreled with the unruly gang of giants. Finally they attacked and killed Ymir, the father of them all.

Immense floods of blood spurted from the fallen giant and drowned all the frost giants except BERGELMIR and his wife, who rode out the flood on a hollowed tree trunk, the first boat.

The brothers dragged Ymir's huge body to Ginnungagap, and there they set about creating the world. They made the earth from his flesh, mountains and hills from his bones and rocks and boulders from his teeth. His curly hair became leafy trees and all vegetation. The lakes and seas and oceans were made from his blood.

Sky Then they made the sky's dome from his skull and flung his brains aloft to make the

THIS EARLY 17TH-CENTURY PRINT, DEPICTING THE CREATION ACCORDING TO THE OLD TESTAMENT GENESIS, SHOWS ERUPTIONS OF FIRE AND SWIRLING CLOUDS SIMILAR TO THOSE DESCRIBED IN THE NORSE MYTHOLOGY OF THE CREATION.

clouds. Four DWARFS would later be set to hold up the four corners of the sky. Their names were NORDI, SUDRI, AUSTRI and WESTRI. The four points of the compass, North, South, East and West, are named after them. The gods took sparks and embers from Muspellheim's fires and made the sun and moon and stars.

Jotunheim The sons of Bor gave the new generation of giants, the race founded by Bergelmir, the land they named JOTUNHEIM. They bade the giants stay there.

Midgard Then they put Ymir's eyebrows around a green piece of land, forming a pleasant enclosure they called MIDGARD, or Middle Earth.

Night and Day Once the gods had created the world and placed the sun and moon in the sky, they made night and day.

NIGHT (or Nott) was a beautiful giantess with a dark complexion and hair of midnight black. She was the daughter of NARFI, one of the first giants. She married three times. Her first husband was NAGLFARI, father of AUD. Her second was ANNAR, father of EARTH. With her third husband, DELLING (Dawn), she had a fair son named DAY.

The gods sent Night and Day up into the heavens in horse-drawn chariots to ride around the world. They created darkness and light, as one followed the other through the skies.

Night drove first, with her lead horse FROSTY MANE (HRIMFAXI). The froth from his bit fell to earth as dewdrops.

After Night came Day with his horse, SHINING MANE (SKINFAXI). His golden glow lighted up the heavens and the earth.

Sun and Moon The gods placed the sun and the moon in chariots, to be drawn by splendid horses. The horses were driven by SOL and MANI, the daughter and the son of a man from MIDGARD whose name was MUNDILFARI. He had named his beautiful children after the sun and moon in the sky. The gods were angry at his pride and had stolen his children away.

Sol's horses were ARVAKR (Early Waker) and ALSVID (All-Swift). A shield, SVALIN, was placed in Sol's chariot to protect her from the direct rays of the sun, whose brilliant rays would have burned her to a cinder.

Mani's horse was ALDSVIDER (Rapid Goer).

Mani, the man of the moon, stole two more earth children to help him drive his chariot. Their names were BIL and YUKI. The shadows we see on the face of the moon are said to be those of the moon children, carrying a pail of water between them on a pole.

Sun and Moon could never pause in their journeys across the heavens, for they were forever pursued by the terrible wolves SKOLL and HATI. Each month Hati takes a bite out of the moon and tries to gobble it up. But the moon escapes and grows whole again. In the end the wolves will devour both sun and moon and cast the world into darkness at RAGNAROK, the end of the world.

The First Humans The first man was ASK (Ash) and the first woman, EMBLA (Elm). They were created by the first three AESIR gods, ODIN, VILI and VE. This is how it happened:

The gods were walking along the seashore when they saw two tree trunks lying at the edge of the water. The forms of the trees were beautiful. Odin breathed life into them. Vili gave them the ability to speak and think. Ve gave them warmth and color and movement.

The gods gave them MIDGARD in which to live. All human beings were descended from them. (See "Rig-Heimdall," under HEIMDALL, who created the different races of men and women.)

The Dwarfs The gods made gnomes and DWARFS from the grubs in Ymir's rotting corpse. They gave them human form and endowed them with brains, but they were ugly, misshapen little creatures, greedy and selfish. The gods gave them SVARTALFHEIM, the dark realm underground, and put them in charge of the earth's treasures of gold, precious metals and gems. The dwarfs were master smiths. (See THE TREASURES OF THE DWARFS.)

Asgard Now that the earth was made and filled with DWARFS and giants and humans, the gods created for themselves the beautiful realm of ASGARD, home of the AESIR gods. It was linked to MIDGARD by the Rainbow Bridge, BIFROST, and it was sheltered by the great World Tree, YGGDRASIL, which touched upon all the worlds.

The story of the Creation is from SNORRI STURLUSON's PROSE EDDA, his major sources being "VOLUSPA," "The Lay of Grimnir," and "VAFTRUDNISMAL."

D

DAIN One of the two DWARFS who fashioned FREYA's gold-bristled boar, HILDISVINI. The other dwarf was NABBI.

DAY The son of NIGHT and her third husband, DELLING. ODIN set Night and her son, Day, in the sky to ride around the world, bringing darkness and light at regular intervals. Day's horse was SHINING MANE (SKINFAXI) whose golden glow lighted up the earth. (See "Night and Day," under CREATION.)

DELLING (Dawn or Dayspring) The third husband of NIGHT. Their son was called DAY. Delling was related to the sons of Bor, the gods ODIN, VILI and VE. (See "Night and Day," under CREATION.)

DRAGON A mythical beast, usually represented as a large, winged, fire-breathing reptile similar to a crocodile or a SERPENT. It played an important part in the folklore of many peoples around the world, so its physical characteristics vary. In the Middle Ages it was a symbol for sin and paganism. Saint George, patron saint of England, is often depicted slaying a dragon. In Norse myth the dragon NITHOG feeds on the root of the World Tree, YGGDRASIL. In Norse and Germanic legend the dragon FAFNIR guards his ill-gotten treasure and is eventually slain by the young hero SIEGFRIED. However, in some countries such as China, the dragon is a symbol of good fortune. In many cities paper dragons are paraded through the streets at Chinese New Year.

DRAUPNIR (Dropper) The golden ring or arm ring made for the great god ODIN by the dwarfs SINDRI and BROKK. (See THE TREASURES OF THE DWARFS.) Every ninth night eight other rings dropped from Draupnir, each as heavy and bright as the first.

In the story "Frey and Gerda," (see under FREY), Gerda was not tempted by the ring; in "Balder's Funeral," (see under BALDER), Odin placed Draupnir on the funeral pyre; it was then returned to him by HERMOD, the messenger god who had gone to the underworld to try to get Balder back to the living.

DROMI One of the chains with which the gods tried to bind the wolf, FENRIS.

DVALIN The DWARF who, with his three brothers, ALFRIGG, BERLING and GRERR, fashioned the golden BRISINGS' NECKLACE coveted by the goddess FREYA. (See "Freya and the Golden Necklace," under FREYA.) The other three dwarfs are never heard of again, but Dvalin was turned into stone by the rising sun. (See ALVIS.)

"DVALIN'S DELIGHT" The ironic name given by the DWARFS to the sun. Dwarfs, gnomes, trolls and other denizens of underground caves are terrified of the sun, for it turns them into stone. They must never be caught aboveground in daylight. (See ALVIS.)

DWARFS The small, misshapen creatures made at the CREATION from the grubs in the giant YMIR's dead body. They were given the realm of SVARTALFHEIM (land of the dark ELVES) in which to live. The gods put them in charge of the earth's underground treasures: precious metals and gems. They were master craftsmen and fashioned many treasures for the gods. (See THE TREASURES OF THE DWARFS.)

The PROSE EDDA lists dozens of names of dwarfs, but few of them are ever heard of again in the myths. Among the memorable ones are:

- ALVIS, who like many of the dwarfs had a vast store of knowledge and poetically listed the various names for the 13 most important words in medieval Scandina-

Siegfried, hero of Germanic legend, slays the dragon Fafnir.

vian vocabulary. (See "Words of Alvis," under ALVIS).

- BROKK and SINDRI, who fashioned various gifts for the gods. (See THE TREASURES OF THE DWARFS.)
- DVALIN, one of the dwarfs who made the BRISINGS' NECKLACE coveted by the goddess FREYA and who was turned into stone at sunrise.
- ANDVARI, the dwarf who was tricked by LOKI into giving up his gold hoard upon which he then placed a curse. (See "Otter's Ransom," under OTTER.)
- LIT, the dwarf who inadvertently got cremated on BALDER's funeral pyre.
- NORDI, SUDRI, AUSTRI and WESTRI, the four dwarfs who were bidden to hold up the four corners of the sky. (See "Sky," under CREATION.)

All the countries of northwestern Europe have some form of "little people" in their folklore, variously called trolls, GOBLINS, pucks, bogies, spriggans, kobolds, brownies and other colorful names, sometimes varying from one district to another no more than a few miles away. Some of them are kind and helpful to humans, as in the fairy tale "Snow White and the Seven Dwarfs;" some are malicious, as in Christina Rossetti's poem "Goblin Market"; some were supposed to steal human babies and leave their own wizened changelings in their place. Some scholars account for the numerous superstitions about "the little folk" by conjecturing that there was once a race of small, dark people in northern countries who were driven underground and into the hills by invading tribes of larger people.

DEEP UNDER THE EARTH, DWARFS CRAFTED METALS AND GEMS INTO TREASURES FOR THE GODS AND GODDESSES.

E

EARLY WAKER (Arvakr) One of the two horses that draws the SUN chariot driven by the fair maiden SOL. (See "Sun and Moon," under CREATION.) The other horse is ALL-SWIFT (ALSVID).

EARTH MOTHER or EARTH GODDESS A general name for a spirit or deity worshiped by primitive peoples all over the world. People prayed to her for fine weather and good crops, for food and shelter and for numerous sons and daughters. In Norse mythology the first earth goddesses had no distinct form, but later were identified with FJORGIN, FRIGG and FREYA.

THE EDDAS Two distinct works, the *Elder* or POETIC EDDA (see under POETIC EDDA) and the *Younger* or PROSE EDDA, sometimes known as the *Snorra Edda* (see under PROSE EDDA). The eddas are our main source of knowledge about Norse mythology.

The *Poetic Edda* is a collection of poems on mythological and legendary themes, written down at different times and by different poets between the 8th and 13th centuries. They were not discovered until 1643 by the Icelandic bishop Sveinsson. (The *Poetic Edda* was sometimes called "Saemund's Edda" in the mistaken belief that it had been written by medieval Bishop Saemund.)

The *Prose Edda*, "younger" because it wasn't written until around 1220, was written by Icelandic poet, historian and diplomat SNORRI STURLUSON (1179–1241). It is a handbook of Norse mythology, designed as a guide for poets to encourage them to write in the style of the ancient poets of the Viking Age.

These two great books helped to keep alive the memory of the ancient gods and their exploits, which otherwise might have been lost forever with the coming of Christianity to the northern lands.

EGGTHER Watchman of the giants. At RAGNAROK, the end of the world, he sits upon a grave mound and grimly plays upon his harp.

EINHERIAR The dead warriors resurrected in Odin's VALHALLA to fight all day and feast all night, in preparation for RAGNAROK, the end of the world.

EITRI Another name for SINDRI, the DWARF.

ELDER EDDA See POETIC EDDA.

ELDHRIMNIR (Soot Blackened) The name of the cauldron at VALHALLA in which the magic boar, SAEHRIMNIR, was cooked every night for the feasting of the gods and heroes.

ELDIR (Man of Fire) One of the servants of AEGIR, the sea god.

ELIVAGAR The collective name for 11 venomous rivers that surge from the spring HVERGELMIR in the underworld, NIFLHEIM. The rivers have fearsome names that relate to howling and boiling and storming: Svol, Gunnthra, Fjorm, Fimbulthul, Slid, Hrid, Sylg, Ylg, Leipt, Gjoll and Vid. The rivers freeze into ice and roar into GINNUNGAGAP, the abyss, as glaciers. The first giant, YMIR, was formed from the frozen poison of the Elivagar. (See CREATION.)

In the story "Thor's Duel with Hrungnir" (see under THOR), Thor tells of carrying AURVANDIL in a basket across the Elivagar.

In the story "Thor and Hymir Go Fishing" (see under THOR), Thor and TYR journey to the east of the Elivagar in Thor's goat chariot.

ELLI, ELLE Old Age in the form of an old woman with whom the god THOR wrestled at UTGARD-LOKI's hall. Thor was, of course, defeated, for no one can win against old age. (See "Thor's Journey to Utgard," under THOR.)

ELVES (singular, elf) In some tales elves were beautiful ghostlike creatures with magical powers. In Norse mythology elves don't play an active part; they are mentioned only in passing. For example, the Vanir god FREY was sometimes called lord of the elves. The domain of the elves was ALFHEIM. When the dwarf ALVIS cites the 13 most important words in the language, he mentions the elves only twice. In some accounts of Balder's funeral (see under BALDER) the elves came to mourn, along with the gods, giants and dwarfs. The Dark Elves, whose domain was SVARTALFHEIM, seem to be indistinguishible from DWARFS.

EMBLA The first woman, who was created from an alder or elm tree by the first three AESIR gods, ODIN, VILI and VE. (See "The First Humans," under CREATION.) In Norse myth all human beings were descended from Embla and ASK, the first man.

F

FAFNIR Son of the magician REIDMAR and brother of REGIN and OTTER. Fafnir killed his father for his hoard of gold (see "Otter's Ransom," under OTTER), then turned himself into a dragon to guard the gold. He was himself killed by the young hero SIGURD.

In Richard Wagner's 19th-century opera cycle THE RING OF THE NIBELUNG, Fafnir is one of the giants who helps WOTAN (ODIN) to build VALHALLA. He later turns himself into a dragon and is killed by Siegfried (the German name for Sigurd).

FALCON A bird of prey that hunts during the day. Like its relatives the hawk and the eagle, it has extraordinary eyesight and powers of flight. In mythology birds such as falcons are often thought of as bearing a person's spirit into other worlds. In Norse mythology the goddess FREYA possessed a suit of falcon feathers that enabled her to travel wherever she wanted.

Freya lent her suit of feathers to LOKI so that he might rescue IDUNN (see "Idunn's Apples," under IDUNN) and again in "The Theft of Thor's Hammer," so that he might find MJOLLNIR, the hammer (see under THOR). On another occasion, in "Thor and the Giant Geirrod," Loki borrowed a falcon suit from FRIGGA, the wife of ODIN.

FARBAUTI (Cruel Striker) A giant, or JOTUN, the father of the trickster god, LOKI. Loki's mother was the giantess LAUFEY or Nal, according to the PROSE EDDA. Some say that Farbauti struck Laufey with a bolt of lightning, after which she gave birth to Loki.

FATES See NORNS.

FENRIS (Fenrir) The wolf who was the creation of the trickster god, LOKI, and the ogress ANGERBODA. He was the brother of HEL and of JORMUNGAND, the MIDGARD SERPENT. Fenris was so huge that when he opened his mouth, his jaws stretched from Earth to heaven. He was bound by the gods (see below) and doomed to remain in chains until RAGNAROK (the end of the world), when he would kill the great god ODIN. He in turn would then be killed by VIDAR, one of Odin's sons.

Fenris and the Gods FENRIS, the creation of LOKI and ANGERBODA, was so huge and hairy that the AESIR (the gods of ASGARD) were frightened of him. Only TYR was brave enough to befriend the monster wolf and feed him. But as Fenris grew bigger and bigger, the gods decided he should be chained. One chain was called LAEDING, another, DROMI. Fenris easily broke the chains. Then the gods sent SKIRNIR, the servant of the god FREY, to seek the help of the DWARFS, who lived in the earth.

The dwarfs fashioned a silken bond (called GLEIPNIR) from:

- the sound of a cat's paws
- the hairs of a maiden's beard
- the roots of a mountain
- the dreams of a bear
- the breath of a fish
- the spittle of a bird

Because none of these things seem to exist on earth, the bond that was forged could not be broken by anyone or anything on earth.

The gods persuaded Fenris to go with them to a lonely island (Lyngvi, in the middle of Lake Amsvartnir). They asked Fenris if he would allow himself to be tied up once more and use his mighty strength to break the bond.

For all his fearsome ways, Fenris was a sporting wolf. He agreed to be bound if one of the gods would put a hand into Fenris's mouth as a guarantee that the wolf would be set free no matter what.

Tyr, the most fair-minded of the gods, agreed to put his hand into Fenris's mouth.

FENRIS, THE MONSTER WOLF, BIT OFF THE HAND OF THE GOD TYR.

Fenris could not break the bond. He clamped down on Tyr's hand in pain, and Tyr lost his hand.

The gods then attached Gleipnir to a heavy chain called GELGIA, and passed the chain through a hole into a large rock called GIOLL. Then one of the gods thrust his sword into the wolf's mouth so that it would remain agape. Thus Fenris was bound and gagged. His dreadful howls would be heard until the fatal day of RAGNAROK.

The fate of Fenris was cruel, but for the Norsemen the wolf was very real and very frightening, an ever-present danger in their world and the villain of many a horror story. Because Fenris was also a supernatural creature of enormous size and strength, it is no wonder that the gods were terrified of him and decided to put him out of the way. Fenris got his revenge at Ragnarok, when he would kill the chief god, ODIN.

SNORRI STURLUSON's vivid version of this myth in the PROSE EDDA is the only surviving source.

FENSALIR (Sea or Water Hall) The hall of the goddess FRIGGA.

FIMAFENG (the Swift) One of the servants of AEGIR, the sea god. He was stabbed to death by the trickster god, LOKI, at Aegir's banquet for the gods. (See "Loki's Mocking," under LOKI.)

FIMBUL WINTER, FIMBULVETR The winter of winters, the worst of all possible winters; it lasted for three years without respite and was the forerunner of RAGNAROK, the end of the world. It brought terrible hardships, with driving snowstorms from all four points of the compass, vicious winds, bitter cold, unyielding ice. People starved and lost all hope and goodness, fighting for their lives. Terrible crimes were committed and wars ensued.

FJALAR (1) (All-Knower) The rooster that crows to the giants at the beginning of RAGNAROK, the end of the world.

FJALAR (2) One of the wicked DWARFS who killed KVASIR, the wise man. (See "The Mead of Poetry," under ODIN.)

FJOLSVID The giant who guarded the gate in JOTUNHEIM behind which the fair MENGLAD waited for her lover, SVIPDAG.

FJORGYN Also known as Jord or Earth, she was an earth goddess, mother of FRIGGA. In "The Lay of Harbard," (see under HARBARD) she is referred to as the mother of THOR.

FLOOD At the time of CREATION in Norse mythology, the giant YMIR was killed by the gods. His spurting blood created a flood. All the giants were drowned except BERGELMIR and his wife, who created a new race of giants. Oceans, seas and lakes were formed from Ymir's blood. In the Old Testament Bible (Genesis), Noah and his family and animals are the only survivors of a flood. Stories of floods occur in many mythologies around the world, from India and Russia to New Guinea and North and South America.

FOLKVANGER (Field of Folk) The part of ASGARD in which the hall of the goddess FREYA was situated. In the hall, SESSRUMNIR, she welcomed the slain heroes that she shared with ODIN.

FORSETI God of justice and conciliation. He was the son of BALDER and NANNA. His hall was GLITNIR. Not much is known about Forseti, but place names such as Forsetlund, near Oslo Fjord in Norway, suggest that he once may have been an important god.

FREKI (Greedy) One of the wolf companions of the god ODIN. The other was GERI, whose name also means "greedy." Odin fed the wolves all the meat that was given to him, for he needed only to drink divine MEAD to survive. The wolves attended him at HLIDSKIALF, his high seat, and also at VALHALLA.

FREY, FREYR One of the great gods of the Norsemen. His name means "Lord" (as his sister FREYA's means "Lady"). He was the lord of the sun, rain and harvests. He was a shining god, bringing fertility and prosperity to all. Son of the VANIR god NIORD, Frey was one of the hostages asked to live in ASGARD after THE WAR BETWEEN THE AESIR AND THE VANIR. His home was ALFHEIM (elfland), and he was sometimes known as lord of the elves.

Among THE TREASURES OF THE DWARFS that went to Frey were the ship SKIDBLADNIR (Wooden Slats), which could carry all the gods and their horses and armor and yet be folded small enough to fit in a pouch; the golden boar GULLINBURSTI (Golden Bristles), who plowed the earth and made it green; and a magic sword that struck out at JOTUNS and trolls of its own accord. Frey gave this sword as a BRIDAL PRICE to GERDA's father, GYMIR (See "Frey and Gerda," below.) He would regret its loss at RAG-NAROK (Doomsday), when he was to battle with the fire demon SURT and lose his life.

Frey wed Gerda after his servant SKIRNIR had wooed her for him. Many scholars interpret the story "Frey and Gerda" as a legend about the wooing of the frozen earth (Gerda) by the warm sun (Frey).

Historically, the worship of Frey was widespread and persistent, especially among the Swedes. At around the year 1200 there was a magnificent statue of Frey (called there Fricco, The Lover) alongside the two other great gods, ODIN and THOR, in Uppsala, Sweden.

Frey and Gerda Frey was one of the most celebrated of the gods. He was the god of fertility, peace and wealth.

One myth has it that Frey dared to climb onto the great god ODIN's high seat, HLIDSKIALF,

FREY ASTRIDE HIS GOLDEN BOAR, GULLINBURSTI.

where no one but Odin, and sometimes his wife, FRIGGA, was allowed to sit. From this aerie Odin could see all the NINE WORLDS.

Frey looked about him and his gaze was transfixed by a dazzling vision. He had seen GERDA, the fair daughter of the giant GYMIR. As she opened the gates to her palace, her shapely arms shone with such radiance that the earth and the sky around her shimmered with light.

Frey left Odin's palace feeling sad and desolate. He knew that because Gerda was a JOTUN, a daughter of one of the hated giants, and he, Frey, was lord of the elves, he could never win her. And besides, it was said that her heart was as frozen as a seed in the hard winter earth.

Frey was so unhappy that he couldn't eat or sleep or speak. Everyone was troubled for him; trees lost their leaves and flowers faded. All nature mourned for Frey. At last Frey's father, NIORD, sent SKIRNIR ("the shining one") to speak to his son.

Skirnir was Frey's friend and trusted servant. It didn't take him long to find out what troubled Frey.

Skirnir said that he would go to woo the maiden for Frey if Frey would lend him BLOODYHOOF, the wondrous horse that could leap through fire unharmed, and his magic sword that struck giants and trolls of its own accord.

Frey agreed and Skirnir set off to JOTUNHEIM, the land of the giants. When he came to a wall of fire, Bloodyhoof leapt with Skirnir through the flames. They both came out unscathed.

Outside Gymir's hall huge hounds set up a fearsome barking, howling like the winds of winter. Skirnir asked an old shepherd for advice, but the man offered no help. He told Skirnir that he had no hope of winning Gerda, for her heart was made of ice. He said that Frey was doomed to failure and death.

But Skirnir knew that the NORNS had decided his fate and when he should die. There was nothing he could do except to go about his duty with hope and courage.

Inside her hall, Gerda looked coldly at Skirnir. First he offered her golden apples if she would give her love to Frey. But Gerda had plenty of gold.

Then he offered her Odin's magic ring, DRAUPNIR. But Gerda had plenty of jewels.

Then Skirnir tried threats. He would cut off her head with the magic sword. Gerda said that her father would kill Skirnir first and keep the magic sword for himself.

Now Skirnir drew from his belt a wand and a knife. He said he would carve the most terrifying magic RUNES upon the wand and strike her with it. The runes would be curses that doomed her to be forever lonely and filled with longing. She would have no friends, no husband, no children. Only the horrible frost giant HRIMGRIMNIR would pursue her with foul corpses for companions. Food and drink would taste loathsome to her. She would always be cold and miserable, and would slowly dry up like a dying thistle, trampled underfoot and forgotten by all.

At this dreadful threat Gerda at last promised to marry Frey. Skirnir left Frey's magic sword behind as a BRIDE PRICE for Gymir, and rode back to Frey with the happy news that Gerda would wed him in nine days at the sacred barley patch, BARRI. (In Norse mythology nine days symbolize the nine months of a northern winter.) Frey was dismayed by the long delay until he should meet his bride.

It is said that after they were married Frey and Gerda were the happiest couple in the world, for the warmth of Frey's love had melted Gerda's icy heart, just as the sun of spring thaws the frozen earth and brings forth the plants from seeds hidden inside it.

The story of Frey and Gerda is a moving love poem; it exemplifies the deep longing Norsemen had for the sunshine and warmth of spring after the long, frozen winters of their native lands.

FREYA (Lady) The goddess of love and fertility. She was the daughter of the VANIR god, NIORD, and his sister-wife, NERTHUS, and the sister of FREY. Freya came to ASGARD with her brother and father after THE WAR BETWEEN THE AESIR AND VANIR ended in an eternal peace treaty.

Freya's home in Asgard was in FOLKVANGER in a hall called SESSRUMNIR.

Freya was married to ODUR (or OD), but this mysterious character (whose name means "roamer") disappeared; Freya was said to roam the earth looking for him and shedding tears that turned to pure gold. Freya and Odur had a daughter named HNOSSA. Her name means "jewel."

Freya was exceedingly beautiful and many fell in love with her, including giants (see "The Theft of Thor's Hammer," under THOR; "Asgard's Wall and the Giant Builder," under ASGARD, and "Thor's Duel with Hrungnir," under THOR), dwarfs (see "Freya and the Golden Necklace," below) and men (see "Freya, Ottar and the Giantess Hyndla," below).

Like most of the Vanir, Freya had a talent for witchcraft. It is said that when she came to Asgard, she instructed the gods about magic charms and potions. In "Freya, Ottar and the Giantess Hyndla," below, we see Freya using her magic on HYNDLA by creating a ring of flame around her.

Freya also had a warlike side and shared ODIN's love of battle. It is said that she and Odin divided the slain heroes between them, so that some went to Odin's VALHALLA while others were chosen by Freya to be entertained at her hall, Sessrumnir. Freya's boar, the gold-bristled HILDISVINI, was a symbol of war. Its name means "Battle Boar."

As well as a boar chariot, Freya had a chariot pulled by two gray or black cats.

She had a falcon skin that she sometimes donned to fly away. She lent the falcon skin to LOKI, the trickster god, in the stories of "Idunn's

FREYA HAD A CHARIOT PULLED BY TWO CATS.

Apples" (see under IDUNN) and "The Theft of Thor's Hammer" (see under THOR).

The sixth day of the week, FRIDAY, is named after Freya.

Her most precious possession was the BRIS-INGS' NECKLACE. See "Freya and the Golden Necklace," below.

Freya, Ottar and the Giantess Hyndla

Freya, goddess of love and fertility, was loved by many, including the human male, OTTAR. In "The Lay of Hyndla" from the POETIC EDDA, Freya goddess of love, transforms her lover Ottar into the shape of her boar, HILDISVINI, and visits the giantess HYNDLA in her cave. Hyndla is a powerful seeress. Freya cajoles and bullies her into telling Ottar all about his ancestors from far back, so that he may win a wager with another mortal, Angantyr. In Norse times, as in biblical times, it was very important to know one's lineage; proof of it was often used to settle disputes over land and other property. One of Ottar's ancestors turned out to be SIGURD, the greatest of Germanic heroes, so he was sure to win his bet.

When Hyndla has finished reciting the list of Ottar's ancestors, she wanted to leave Freya and her "boar." Freya used witchcraft to persuade Hyndla to brew some "memory beer" for Ottar, so that he will remember every detail of what she has told him. Freya caused flames to dance around the giantess until she gave Ottar the brew.

Freya and the Golden Necklace

Freya, goddess of love and fertility, had an enormous greed for gold and jewelry of all kinds. She could never have enough. One day she went to the cave of the black DWARFS DVALIN, ALFRIGG, BERLING and GRERR. These master craftsmen had made a golden necklace of outstanding beauty. Freya knew at once that she would do anything to get the necklace that the dwarfs called the BRIS-INGS' NECKLACE.

She offered the dwarfs gold and silver but, as Dvalin pointed out, they already had all the precious metals and gems of the underworld for the taking.

Freya wept golden tears. At last Dvalin said that they would give her the necklace if she would agree to spend a day and a night with each of the dwarfs. Freya was so overcome with greed that she gave herself to the company of the four ugly little creatures for four days and four nights. When she went back to her palace at FOLKVANGER, she was wearing the Brisings' Necklace around her throat.

Now LOKI, the mischiefmaker, had followed Freya to SVARTALFHEIM, the home of the dwarfs, and had seen everything that had happened. He ran to tell ODIN. Odin was furious when he heard the story. He bade Loki to take the necklace from Freya and bring it to him.

Loki had a hard time getting into Freya's sleeping chamber at SESSRUMNIR, her palace, for all the doors and windows were tightly shut. At last the shape-changer turned himself into a small fly and entered the room through a hole as small as a needle's eye. Then Loki saw that Freya was wearing the necklace around her neck, with the clasp underneath her, so that he couldn't reach it. Never at a loss, Loki turned himself into a flea and bit the goddess on her cheek. She turned restlessly in her sleep and the clasp was exposed. Quickly Loki turned back into his own shape, removed the necklace, unlocked the door and crept out.

When Freya discovered her loss she ran to Odin and told her story, weeping bitterly.

Cold with anger at Freya's tale of greed and lust, Odin said that he would retrieve the jewel for her only if she would agree to stir up a terrible war between two powerful chieftains on earth. He demanded that there should be killing and bloodshed. Afterward Freya should bring the slain heroes back to life. Freya willingly agreed to the terms, for like Odin, she had the gift of sorcery and a lust for battle and heroes. In fact, she shared the slain heroes with Odin and entertained half of them at Sessrumnir, while the other half feasted at Odin's VALHALLA.

Then Odin sent for HEIMDALL, the watchman of the gods, and told him to go after Loki and bring back Freya's trinket.

Loki turned himself into a seal and swam to a rock near SINGASTEIN. But a moment later Heimdall, too, had become a seal. The two fought a fierce battle. In the end Heimdall, with the necklace in his hand, led the dripping Loki out of the water and back to Odin.

The story of the BRISINGS' NECKLACE is from

FREYA VISITED THE DWARFS TO OBTAIN HER GOLDEN NECKLACE.

the 15th-century *Flateyjarbok* ("Book of the Flat Island") and from the 10th-century scaldic poem *Husdrapa*.

FRIDAY In English, Friday, the sixth day of the week, takes its name from FREYA, the Norse goddess of love and fertility. In Latin, French, Italian and Spanish Friday was also named after a goddess of love, Venus of Roman mythology. Friday is *dies Veneris* (Venus's Day) in Latin, *vendredi* in French, *venerdí* in Italian and *viernes* in Spanish.

FRIGGA (FRIGG, FRIJA, FRICKA) The chief AESIR goddess; wife of ODIN; daughter of FJORGIN, the goddess of earth; Frigga herself is called EARTH MOTHER. She is associated with love, marriage and motherhood. She is frequently pic-

tured as being very beautiful, wearing a girdle hung with household keys and weaving clouds on her spinning wheel. She had 11 handmaidens who attended her in her hall, FENSALIR. She was the mother of BALDER, the golden god whose death preceded RAGNAROK, the end of the world. According to some sources, Frigga was also the mother of THOR, the thunder god, and of HODUR, the blind god who unwittingly slew Balder. In Richard Wagner's 19th-century opera THE RING OF THE NIBELUNG, she is named Fricka.

Because of the fragmentary nature of the Norse eddas and sagas, there are conflicting views of Frigga. Besides appearing as a devoted wife and mother, Frigga also appears as a sorceress who wears a falcon skin and sees into the future, and as a wanton woman who covets gold and jewelry and the love of men (see "Loki's Mocking," under LOKI). She and the goddess FREYA have a lot in common. Some believe that they are various facets of the same deity.

FROST GIANTS See JOTUN.

FROSTY MANE (HRIMFAXI) The lead horse of NIGHT's team, who each morning sprinkles the ground below with dew shed from his bridle. (See "Night and Day," under CREATION.)

FRIGGA, ATTENDED BY HER HANDMAIDENS, SPUN CLOUDS ON HER SPINDLE.

FYLGIE (follower) As well as the NORNS, or Fates, the Norsemen ascribed to each human being a guardian spirit or double, which stayed with a person throughout his or her life. The fylgie had a human or other animal shape but was invisible except in dreams or at the moment of death. If the fylgie appeared to a person who was awake, it presaged that person's death. When a person dies, the fylgie passes on to another member of the family.

G

GALAR One of the two DWARFS (the other was FJALAR) who killed the wise man KVASIR and collected his blood to make the Mead of Poetry (see under ODIN).

GAGNRAD One of the many names assumed by the god ODIN. He used this one when he went to visit the wise giant, VAFTRUDNIR.

GANG One of the storm giants, brother of THIAZZI and IDI, son of OLVALDI, who had left piles of gold to be divided among his sons. (See "Skade and Niord," under SKADE.)

GANGLATI One of HEL's slow-moving servants who served in ELJUDNIR, Hel's hall in the underworld.

GANGLOT One of HEL's slow-moving servants who served in ELJUDNIR, Hel's hall in the underworld.

GARM The fearsome, howling hound who stood at the gates of HEL, guarding the kingdom of the dead. In some tellings, he could be quieted only by a piece of cake given to him by those who had given bread to the poor. In "The Lay of Grimnir" Garm is described as the fiercest of all hounds; in "Balder's Dreams" (see under BALDER), when ODIN went to the underworld to consult a seeress, the blood-caked hound of Hel howled at him, but Odin went on, undeterred by the hideous noise; at RAGNAROK Garm fought with one-handed TYR and they killed each other. Garm is sometimes thought to be another name for the wolf FENRIS.

GEFION (Giver) A goddess of fertility, associated with the plow. In one myth told by SNORRI STURLUSON in the PROSE EDDA, Gefion disguised herself as a beggarwoman. She asked GYLFI, the king of Sweden, to give her some land. The king told her that she could have as much land as she could plow in a day and a night. The old woman went off to find her four sons, who were huge oxen that had been fathered by a giant. Gefion hitched the oxen to a plow and proceeded to cut deeply into the land of Sweden. Then she and the oxen towed the land into the sea where it is now known as the Danish island of Zealand.

GEIRROD (1) The giant who, with the help of the trickster LOKI, persuaded the god THOR to visit him without his famous weapons. Thanks to the friendly giantess GRID, Thor was able to kill Geirrod and his two ogress daughters, GIALP and GREIP. (See "Thor and the Giant Geirrod," under THOR.)

GEIRROD (2) Son of King HRAUDING, brother of AGNAR. Geirrod betrayed his brother and took his throne. Later he killed himself by falling upon his own sword, as ODIN, his benefactor, had prophesied in his "Grimnirsmal" (or "Lay of Grimnir"). (See "Geirrod and Agnar," below.)

Geirrod and Agnar The two brothers were the sons of King HRAUDING of the Goths. When the children were eight and ten years old, respectively, their little fishing boat was wrecked in a storm. The boys landed on an island and were taken care of by an old couple, who were ODIN and FRIGGA in disguise. Frigga took special care of AGNAR and Odin of GEIRROD, giving them many words of advise before sending them back to their own land. As their boat approached shore, Geirrod leapt out, taking the oars with him, and shoved the boat out to sea. Geirrod was welcomed back to his home and, because his father had died, he became king in place of Agnar, who was presumed dead.

Many years went by before Odin and Frigga thought about the two boys they had rescued from the sea. Then Odin boasted that his foster son, Geirrod, was king of a great country, while Frigga's Agnar was a nobody who lived in a cave. Frigga retorted that Geirrod was mean and treacherous. When Odin decided to go to MID-GARD to test Geirrod, Frigga sent her maidservant, Fulla, to warn Geirrod that he was not to trust the visitor who was coming to him, wearing a sky-blue cape.

Geirrod heeded the warning. Odin did wear a sky-blue cape. He called himself GRIMNIR, but more than that he would not say. In a fit of rage at what he considered insolence, Geirrod had Grimnir slung between two fires. And there he stayed for eight days and nights, without food or drink. Then Agnar, the son of Geirrod, named after his lost uncle, took pity on Odin-Grimnir and quenched his thirst with ale.

Grimnir then began to chant a song that was known as "GRIMNIRSMAL" or "The Lay of Grimnir." The song contained a great deal of knowledge about ASGARD, the home of the gods, and about the gods themselves and their possessions, and especially about Odin and his many names. When Geirrod finally realized that his captive was Odin, he leapt up to release him. But he fell upon his own sword and killed himself.

Then Odin disappeared, and Agnar became king and ruled for many peaceable years.

The story of the brothers Geirrod and Agnar and of their relationship with Odin in their childhood adventure serves as a dramatic introduction and ending for the song.

GELGIA The chain to which the gods attached GLEIPNIR, the silken bond created by the DWARFS to capture the wolf FENRIS.

GERDA, GERD (Enclosed Field) The daughter of the JOTUN GYMIR and AURBODA (possibly ANGERBODA, the ogress wife of LOKI), and the sister of BELI. Gerda was wooed and won by the god FREY and his servant SKIRNIR. She spurned apples and gold but finally gave in at the terrible threat of eternal cold and loneliness, thus personifying winter giving in at last to the warm sunshine of spring. The nine nights of waiting between her consent to become Frey's bride and the actual union is symbolic of the long nine months of hard winter, in northern countries,

before spring arrives. In some mythologies the radiance of Gerda personifies the AURORA BO-REALIS (Northern Lights). (See "Frey and Gerda," under FREY.)

GERI (Greedy) One of the wolf companions of the god ODIN. The other was FREKI, whose name also means "greedy." Odin fed the wolves all the meat that was served to him, for he needed only to drink divine MEAD to survive. The wolves attended him at HLIDSKIALF, his high seat, and also at VALHALLA.

GESTA DANORUM A multivolume, partly mythical history of the Danes by 13th-century scholar SAXO GRAMMATICUS. It is a valuable source of Norse mythology.

GIALAR, GJALLAR (Ringing Horn) The trumpet horn of the god HEIMDALL that can be heard throughout the NINE WORLDS. Heimdall sometimes left Gialar beside the spring of MIMIR. At RAGNAROK, the end of the world, the sound of Gialar would summon gods and men to battle.

Gialar is usually pictured as a *lur*, that is, the ancient bronze trumpet of Scandinavia, dating back to about 1000 B.C. Lurs were made in pairs, twisting in opposite directions so that the two held side by side looked like the horns of a large animal. Some lurs have been excavated from the peat bogs of Denmark and can still be played.

GIALP (or GJALP) (Howler) Daughter of the giant GEIRROD and sister of GREIP. She tried to drown the god THOR and, later, to crush him to death against the roof rafters; but she and her sister were themselves killed by Thor. (See "Thor and the Giant Geirrod," under THOR.)

GIANT See JOTUN.

GILLING The giant killed by the dwarfs EJALAR and GALAR. He was the father of SUT-TUNG. (See "The Mead of Poetry," under ODIN.)

GIMLÉ The court of the gods after the end of the world—see "Regeneration," under RAGNA-ROK. Gimlé is described as being fairer than the sun and roofed in gold. There the rulers would live at peace with each other.

GINNUNGAGAP The gaping pit that lay between NIFLHEIM (the place of mists and ice) and MUSPELLHEIM (the world of raging fire). It existed before land or sea, or heaven or earth. It was here that the first living creatures were formed: YMIR, the first giant, and AUDHUMLA, the cow. See CREATION.

GIOLL The rock to which the bonds of the wolf FENRIS were attached after the gods had captured him.

GIOTUNAGARD, GRIOTUNAGARD, GRJO-TUNAGARDAR (Place of Stones or Stone Fence House) The place where the duel between the god THOR and the giant HRUNGNIR took place. (See "Thor's Duel with Hrungnir," under THOR.)

GLADSHEIM (Joyous Home) The hall in AS-GARD where all the AESIR gods had their high seats. It was thatched in silver and stood in the green plain of IDAVOLL. The principal seat was that of the god ODIN. His seat was VALASK-JALF.

GLEIPNIR The silken bond, with magic properties, fashioned by the DWARFS to bind FENRIS, the wolf. (See "Fenris and the Gods," under FEN-RIS.)

GLITNIR The hall of FORSETI, who was the son of the god BALDER. Forseti dwelt in this hall of gold and silver helping to settle arguments and fights.

GOAT A mammal related to the sheep family. Goats are raised all over the world. They will eat almost any kind of plant and give good milk, flesh, and hair. They have keen eyesight and sense of smell and are playful and friendly. Male goats (rams) can be aggressive. Goats have been domesticated since early times. They can be seen in ancient Egyptian art and are mentioned frequently in the Bible. In Norse mythology the god THOR had a cart drawn by two billygoats, TANNGNIOST and TANNGRISNIR. These goats

could be killed and eaten and then revived again the next day. (See "Thor's Journey to Utgard," under THOR.)

GOBLINS See DWARFS.

GOLDEN MANE The English name for GULL-FAXI, the horse ridden by the giant HRUNGNIR when he was defeated in a race by the god ODIN and his steed, SLEIPNIR. Golden Mane was given to MAGNI, son of the god THOR. (See "Thor's Duel with Hrungnir," under THOR.)

GOTHS A Germanic tribe who in the third and fifth centuries invaded, and settled in, parts of the Roman Empire.

In the story "Geirrod and Agnar," (see under GEIRROD) King HRAUDING was king of the Goths. His son GEIRROD succeeded him.

GREIP (Grasper) Daughter of the giant GEIR-ROD and sister of GIALP. The giant sisters tried to kill the god THOR but were themselves crushed to death by him. (See "Thor and the Giant Geirrod," under THOR.)

Greip was also the name of one of the nine wave maidens who were said to be the mothers of HEIMDALL.

GRERR One of the four dwarfs who made the BRISINGS' NECKLACE for the goddess FREYA. The others were ALFRIGG, BERLING, and DVALIN. (See "Freya and the Golden Necklace," under FREYA.)

GRID The giantess who was one of the wives of the god ODIN and mother of their son, VIDAR. Friendly to the gods, she helped THOR by lending him her magic gloves, girdle and staff when Thor visited the giant GEIRROD (see "Thor and the Giant Geirrod," under THOR). Some legends say that she also made the shoe that Vidar wore at RAGNAROK to slay the wolf FENRIS.

GRIM or GRIMNR One of the god ODIN's many nicknames. It is found in many English place names (Grim's Ditch, Grim's Dyke, Grimsby, Grimesthorpe) and reminds us that northern people believed in Odin and the Norse mythology long after Christianity came to their lands.

GRIMNIR (the Hooded One) One of the god ODIN's many names. When he went to MIDGARD to visit his foster son, GEIRROD, Odin wore a sky-blue, hooded cape. "GRIMNIRSMAL," the song or "Lay of Grimnir," was chanted by Odin while he was held captive at the hall of Geirrod. (See "Geirrod and Agnar," under GEIRROD.)

"GRIMNIRSMAL" ("The Lay of Grimnir")
GRIMNIR, who was the god ODIN in disguise, was captured by GEIRROD and slung between two fires. (See "Geirrod and Agnar," under GEIRROD.) Geirrod's son, AGNAR, quenched Grimnir's thirst with horns of ale, and was rewarded by the song that Grimnir sang.

Grimnir's song told about the halls of the gods in their realm, ASGARD (YDALIR, GLADSHEIM and especially VALHALLA, with details about the hall itself, the cook and the boar and the sooty cauldron in which the boar was cooked to feed the slain heroes of Valhalla); it told of Odin's wolves and ravens and of VALGRIND, Valhalla's outer gate, through which 800 warriors would march, side by side.

The song tells of THRYMHEIM; BREIDABLIK; HEIMDALL'S HIMINBJORG; FREYA'S FOLKVANGER; SESSRUMNIR, where Freya shared the dead heroes with Odin; GLITNIR (the home of FORSETI, son of BALDER); NOATUN, the home of NIORD; and of peaceful VIDI, where the god VIDAR lived.

The song tells more about Valhalla and then names all the rivers of the HVERGELMIR. The song tells how the gods gallop over the Rainbow Bridge, BIFROST, to meet the council at the well of URD. It tells of the World Tree, YGGDRASIL, and of those who prey upon it. It tells the name of the VALKYRIES who wait upon the dead heroes of Valhalla.

The song tells the names of the horses that drew the chariots of the sun and moon. It tells of the terrible wolves that chased the chariots.

The song tells of the giant YMIR and how his flesh and bones and hair created the earth. (See CREATION.)

It tells of THE TREASURES OF THE DWARFS.

And finally the captive Grimnir tells of the many names of Odin. It is then that Geirrod realises that his prisoner is the great god Odin himself. He rises up to release his prisoner but falls upon his own sword and kills himself.

"Grimnirsmal" was a mnemonic poem (a sort of memory bank) for storytellers, poets and minstrels who passed on information about myths, legends and folktales to people from one generation to another, and in different communities all over the country. Much of the information in "Grimnirsmal" is not found elsewhere; it reminds us that much old material has been lost to us forever. "Grimnirsmal" is a poem included in the POETIC EDDA and quoted by SNORRI STURLUSON in his PROSE EDDA.

GROA The wife of AURVANDIL the Brave and mother of SVIPDAG, who visits her for advice in NIFLHEIM after her death in the poem "Svipdagsmal," part of the POETIC EDDA.

In the story "Thor's Duel with Hrungnir," (see under THOR), Groa uses her magic spells to cure Thor's headache but fails to remove the whetstone fragments from his skull.

GULLFAXI (Golden Mane) The giant HRUNGNIR's powerful stallion who was defeated in a horse race by the god ODIN on his steed, eight-legged SLEIPNIR. Gullfaxi was then given to MAGNI, the son of the god THOR. (See "Thor's Duel with Hrungnir," under THOR.)

GULLINBURSTI (Golden Bristles) The golden boar made by the DWARFS BROKK and SINDRI from a pigskin and thousands of pieces of gold wire, and given to the god FREY. (See THE TREASURES OF THE DWARFS.) Frey could ride on the boar or hitch his wagon to it, and Guillinbursti would speed across the earth, sky or sea faster than any horse. Its golden rays shone like the sun and made plants grow everywhere. With its tusks Gullinbursti raked the earth and showed men how to plow the land.

Warriors wore the image of Frey's golden boar on helmets and shields as protection and good luck. Archaeologists found a 7th-century helmet topped by a boar at Benty Grange, in Derbyshire, England.

See also BOAR.

GULLINKAMBI (Golden Comb) The rooster that crows to the gods and heroes at VALHALLA to tell them that RAGNAROK has begun.

GULLINTANI (Golden Toothed) A name sometimes given to HEIMDALL, who was supposed to have golden teeth and, hence, a dazzling smile.

GULLTOP (Golden Tuft) The horse of the god HEIMDALL.

GULLWEIG or GULLVEIG (Power of Gold) The beautiful witch who came to ASGARD and was probably the cause of THE WAR BETWEEN THE AESIR AND THE VANIR. She was burned three times by the AESIR but rose up each time to cause trouble among the gods. Also called HEID (Shining One), she is thought by most scholars to be an aspect of the VANIR goddess FREYA, who also loved gold (see "Freya and the Golden Necklace," under FREYA) and had magical powers.

GUNGNIR ODIN's magic spear, made by the DWARF sons of IVALDI. It never missed its mark. It was a symbol of Odin as the god of war. Odin flung his spear at the VANIR gods in THE WAR BETWEEN THE AESIR AND THE VANIR; ever afterward this action was imitated by Norse warriors at the start of a battle to invoke Odin's protection in war.

GUNLOD, GUNNLOD Daughter of the giant SUTTUNG, who made her the guardian of the MEAD of poetry, made from the blood of KVASIR. She became the wife of ODIN when he visited the cave in the mountain, HNITBORG, to steal the mead. She bore Odin a child, BRAGI, who went to ASGARD and became the god of poetry and the husband of IDUNN. (See "The Mead of Poetry," under ODIN.)

"GYLFAGINNING" ("The Deception of GYLFI") The name of the first part of the PROSE EDDA.

GYLFI King of Sweden who was tricked by the goddess GEFION into giving her some of his land. In another myth Gylfi goes to ASGARD, the home of the gods, where he meets three beings called High One, Just As High and Third. He questions them about Asgard, its creation, the doings of the gods and goddesses and the end of the world. The three figures answer his questions at length. The poet SNORRI STURLUSON uses this story about Gylfi as a peg on which to hang the opening of the PROSE EDDA, which is called "GYLFAGINNING" ("The Deception of Gylfi").

GYMIR A JOTUN, the father of GERDA, who became the wife of the shining god, FREY. (See "Frey and Gerda," under FREY.)

H

HAMMER, THOR'S See MJOLLNIR.

HARBARD (Gray Beard) One of the god ODIN's many names. In "THE LAY OF HARBARD" Harbard is a ferryman with one eye, a big hat and cape. He arrogantly refuses to take THOR, who doesn't recognize him as Odin, across the sound on his ferry. The two fling insults and taunts at each other, and in the end Thor has to find another way across the water. The poem is interesting mainly for what it reveals about Thor, Odin and their doings. "The Lay of Harbard" ("Harbardsljoth") appears in the *Codex Regius* and a part of it in the *Arnamagnean Codex*. Both of these works are included in the POETIC EDDA.

"HARBARDSLJOTH" ("The Lay of Harbard") See HARBARD.

HATI The terrible wolf, born in IRONWOOD, probably the offspring of the wolf FENRIS, who pursues the chariot of the moon across the heavens and who will devour the moon at the time of RAGNAROK, the end of the world. (See "Sun and Moon," under CREATION.)

HAUSTLONG A poem by Thiodor of Hvini, a 9th- or 10th-century Norwegian poet. It describes pictures painted on a shield, thus is called a shield poem.

The surviving 20 verses of *Haustlong* are preserved in the PROSE EDDA. Thirteen of the verses tell the myth of Idunn and Thiazzi (see under IDUNN); seven describe "Thor's Duel with Hrungnir" (see under THOR). The most vivid part of the poem is considered to be the description of Thor's ride to meet the giant, in which the god's goat-driven chariot caused thunder, lightning and hailstorms on the earth below. Both stories portray gods carrying out bold exploits against the giants of JOTUNHEIM.

"HAVAMAL" ("Words of the High One") A poem, part of the POETIC EDDA. It contains many proverbs and advice on good living from the High One, who is the god ODIN. Some of it is addressed to the mortal LODDFAFNIR. *Havamal* also contains the lament of Odin for BILLING's daughter and the story of how Odin obtained the Mead of Poetry (see under ODIN). The words of wisdom in the *Havamal*, especially in the "Lay of Loddfafnir," tell us a great deal about the ways of the VIKINGS. They were not necessarily the riotous warriors so often portrayed. Instead, they had a sense of the value of life and wisdom; they cherished friendship, loyalty and hospitality; they could endure hardship and even laugh at it; and they admired bravery and fame.

HEID (Shining One) Another name for GULLWEIG.

HEIDRUN (or HEITHRON) The lively she-goat who nibbled the leaves of LAERAD, the tree of VALHALLA. She produced a never-ending supply of MEAD for the gods and heroes at their nightly feasts in ODIN's hall.

HEIMDALL Watchman of the gods. He was mysteriously born of nine mothers and the god ODIN. His mothers must have been nine-times beautiful, for Heimdall himself was tall and handsome, with a dazzling smile full of sunshine. He was sometimes called the god of light, the shining god or the white god.

Heimdall had a wonderful horn called GIALLAR, whose blast could be heard all over the NINE WORLDS, and which Heimdall would blow at RAGNAROK, the end of the world. His horse was called GULLTOP (Golden Tuft), and his sword was HOFUND. He lived in a fortress-like hall called HIMINBJORG (cliffs of heaven).

Heimdall had amazing abilities. His eyesight was so sharp that he could see for 100 miles all around him. Some said he could see even farther, that he had "second sight" that allowed him to see into the future. It is certain that he saw all the comings and goings of those who crossed BIFROST, the Rainbow Bridge that led from ASGARD, the home of the gods, to MIDGARD (Middle Earth).

It was Heimdall who spotted sly LOKI from afar, when the trickster god had stolen FREYA's necklace and escaped with it into the sea, where he changed himself into a sleek seal. Heimdall, too, was able to change his shape. He dived, seallike, into the water, barking and nipping. Heimdall-Seal vanquished Loki-Seal and took the necklace back to Freya. (See "Freya and the Golden Necklace," under FREYA.) He and Loki were enemies ever after that day, and in the end would kill each other at RAGNAROK.

Heimdall was clever too. It was he who had the brilliant idea of sending the thunder god, mighty THOR, to JOTUNHEIM dressed as a girl in bridal dress in order to get back THOR's magic hammer from the giant THRYM, who had stolen it. (See "The Theft of Thor's Hammer," under THOR.)

Heimdall's hearing was so acute and finely tuned that he could hear the grass pushing up from under the earth and the wool growing on a sheep's back. As for sleep, Heimdall needed so little that it seemed he was always awake and alert. It is no wonder that he was chosen to be the watchman of the gods, standing guard at Bifrost, ever on the lookout for marauding giants and other scoundrels who might try to enter Asgard.

One of the best-known stories about Heimdall is the one in which he disguises himself as a mortal man named RIG and goes wandering around Midgard. (See "Rig-Heimdall and the Races of Men," below).

HEIMDALL'S NINE MOTHERS One obscure and fragmented myth, related in the POETIC EDDA, told the following story about the origins of HEIMDALL, the watchman of the bridge BIFROST:

One day when the great god ODIN walked along the seashore, he came across nine beautiful giantesses, sound asleep on the sand. They were the wave maidens, daughters of the sea

god, AEGIR. Their names were Gialp (Yelper), GREIP (Gripper), Egia (Foamer), Augeia (Sand Strewer), Ulfrun (She-Wolf), Aurgiafa (Sorrow-Whelmer), Sindur (Dusk), Iarnsaxa (Iron Sword), and Alta (Fury).

Odin was so enchanted with their beauty that he wedded all nine of them, and together the nine giantesses brought forth a beautiful son named Heimdall.

The nine mothers nurtured their son on the strength of the earth, the moisture of the sea and the heat of the sun. The new god throve so well on this diet that he was soon tall enough and strong enough to hasten to ASGARD, the home of the gods.

There, the gods further endowed Heimdall with marvelously keen senses and a trumpet called GIALLAR, and named him guardian of the Rainbow Bridge, Bifrost.

This story is told in *"The Lay of Hyndla"* (POETIC EDDA).

RIG-HEIMDALL AND THE RACES OF MEN
HEIMDALL was the watchman of the gods. He seldom left his post on BIFROST, the Rainbow Bridge. But one day, at ODIN's suggestion, Heimdall went down to MIDGARD (Middle Earth) disguised as a mortal man. He left behind his horn, GIALAR, his sword and his golden-topped steed, and took the name RIG.

Rig-Heimdall wandered along the seashore at the edge of the world, the same shore where Odin and his brothers had created ASK and EMBLA, the first man and woman. (See "The First Humans," under CREATION.) Heimdall was curious to see how their descendants were faring. When evening came he saw a rickety old hut. Heimdall knocked and the door creaked open. It was dark and smoky inside, but Rig-Heimdall with his keen eyes could see Ai and Edda (Great Grandfather and Great Grandmother) and gave them his golden smile. They shared their miserable meal with him. And Rig-Heimdall was so courteous and friendly that they shared their bed, too, allowing the sweet-talking god to sleep warmly between their two thin bodies. He shared their food and their bed for three days and three nights, then went on his way.

Nine months after the god's visit Edda gave birth to a son. His parents named him Thrall.

HEIMDALL, THE WATCHMAN OF THE GODS, RIDES GULLTOP AND BRANDISHES HIS HORN, GIALLAR.

The boy was sturdy and strong, and grew to be very good at all the hard and heavy chores that laborers must do: chopping wood, digging the earth, building huts, tending the pigs and goats, gathering food, burning peat. When Thrall grew up he married Esne, another hard worker, and their children and their children's children were the peasants and laborers of the world.

Rig-Heimdall could see all this in his mind's eye, for he had second sight, and he was pleased that he had visited Ai and Edda and helped to found the peasant race. He continued on his journey.

The next evening Rig came to a big farm where he found Afi and Amma (Grandfather and Grandmother). Afi's beard was neatly trimmed and Amma's hair was smooth and silvery; they both wore clean and simple clothes. Rig gave them his golden smile. They shared their nourishing meal with him. And Rig-Heim-

dall was so courteous and friendly that they shared their bed, too, allowing the sweet-talking god to sleep warmly between their sturdy bodies. He shared their food and their bed for three days and three nights, then went on his way.

Nine months after the god's visit Amma gave birth to a son. Their parents named him Freeman. The boy was healthy and ruddy, and he grew to be very good at all the work that a proud farmer must do: building fine houses and sturdy barns, learning the skills of the blacksmith and the reaper of corn and the tender of fine animals. When Freeman grew up he married a strapping girl called Hussif. She knew how to spin and how to weave, she sewed a fine seam and she baked good bread. Their children and their children's children became the farmers, landholders and craftsmen of the world.

Rig-Heimdall could see all this in his mind's

eye, for he had second sight, and he was pleased that he had visited Afi and Amma and helped to found the race of farmers, landholders and craftsmen. He continued on his journey.

The next evening Rig came to a great mansion where he found Father Squire and Mother Lady. Their clothes were rich and glittering with jewels. Rig gave them his golden smile and the handsome couple invited him to dinner. A long table was covered with a linen cloth and set with silver wine jugs and goblets and pewter platters. The servants brought in mounds of delicious meats and fruits. Rig was so courteous and friendly that Lady and Squire shared their luxurious bed with him, allowing the sweet-talking god to sleep warmly between their two shapely bodies. Rig shared their food and their bed for three days and three nights, then went on his way.

Nine months after the god's visit Lady gave birth to a son. The parents named him Earl. The boy was tall and handsome, with golden hair and a golden smile, and he grew to be a fine horseman, skilled with both spear and sword as well as with a bow and arrow. When Earl grew up he married a rich and graceful girl called Princess. Her skin was soft and her fingers long. She played beautifully on the lute and her voice was the envy of the nightingale. She made Earl very rich and happy. Their children and their children's children became the kings and queens of many lands of the world.

Rig-Heimdall could see all this in his mind's eye, for he had second sight, and he was pleased that he had visited Squire and Lady and helped to found the race of kings and queens. But before he could return to Asgard to report to Odin on the descendants of Ask and Embla, there was something he must do.

Rig-Heimdall transported himself to the time when Earl was still a young lad. The god appeared before Earl in a forest grove, bringing with him some sticks with strangely carved markings on them. Rig taught Earl, his son, the secrets of the RUNES and much wisdom about the good and evil in the world, so that Earl and his children and grandchildren could become fine and just rulers of their kingdoms.

Now at last Rig-Heimdall was ready to return to Asgard, for his work in Midgard was done and he felt very pleased with himself.

This story, told in *Rigsthula* in the POETIC EDDA, has the repetitive format of a folktale. It gives us a colorful picture of how the three classes of Norsemen lived: the laborers, the more wealthy farmers, and the rich nobility. Not enough is known about the myth to explain why it was Heimdall and not Odin who was designated as the father of men.

HEL (Hela, Hell)   The goddess of death and the underworld, Hel was the daughter of the evil god LOKI and the ogress ANGERBODA. Her brothers were FENRIS, the wolf, and JORMUNGAND, the Midgard Serpent.

According to the PROSE EDDA, Hel was terrible to look at, for one-half of her was greenish black and the other a livid white, with flesh that seemed to be rotting like that of a corpse, and her face was gloomy, grim and sinister.

The great god ODIN cast Hel down to NIFLHEIM, the realm of cold darkness and death. He bade her look after all the wicked and miserable souls who had died of sickness, corruption and old age. (Dead heroes went to Odin's glorious hall, VALHALLA.) Hel's palace was called ELVIDNER, and here she entertained the dead in a grisly kind of way: her table was called Hunger; her knife, Starvation; her bed, Sickness; and the hangings around it, Misfortune.

It was said that in times of famine and plague Hel left her ghastly realm to roam the earth on her three-legged white horse and to rake up the survivors and sweep them with her broom down to Niflheim.

The early Christians so feared Hel that they borrowed her name to describe the place of everlasting torment reserved for the souls of the wicked—Hell.

Although the gods looked upon her with loathing, she had more power than Odin; once someone was in her power, no one, not even Odin, could reclaim that soul unless Hel gave her permission. In the story of BALDER, who was killed and went to Hel, Hel refused to give him up, even though Odin and FRIGGA sent the god HERMOD to plead and bargain with her.

HERMOD   Son of ODIN and FRIGGA. Hermod was bold and brave. It was he who volunteered to go to HEL's underworld and beg her to release his dead brother, BALDER. (See "Hermod's Jour-

HEL, QUEEN OF THE UNDERWORLD, IS SHOWN HERE WITH HER HOUND, GARM.

ney," under BALDER.) In some versions of the myths, Hermod also goes at Odin's bidding to visit the wizard ROSTIOFF in Lapland. (See "Vali, The Avenger," under VALI.) Hermod stands at Odin's side at the gates of VALHALLA to welcome the dead heroes.

HERTHUS See NERTHUS.

HILDISVINI (Battle-Boar) The goddess FREYA's boar. His golden bristles showed the way in the dark. He was created for Freya by the dwarfs DAIN and NABBI. Freya's human lover, OTTAR, takes the form of Hildisvini to visit, with Freya, the giantess HYNDLA. (See "Freya, Ottar and the Giantess Hyndla," under FREYA; and also BOAR.)

HIMINBJORG (Cliffs of Heaven) The home of the god HEIMDALL in ASGARD.

HIMINBRIOTER (Heaven or Sky Bellower) See SKYBELLOWER.

HJUKI See BIL AND YUKI.

HLESEY The island under which the sea giant, AEGIR, and his wife, RAN, lived in their coral cave. It is thought that the actual site of Hlesey may be the island of Laeso, in the Kattegat ("cat's throat"), a strait between the Danish islands of Jutland and Zealand.

HLIDSKIALF, LIDSKJALF (High Seat) ODIN's throne in the aerie of his palace, VALASKIALF in ASGARD, the home of the gods. From here Odin could see what everyone was doing in all the NINE WORLDS. He had his ravens, HUGIN and MUNIN, to help him, and the wolves GERI and FREKI to keep him company. No one but Odin was allowed to sit on Hlidskialf except his wife FRIGGA. But the god FREY once disobeyed the rules. From the high perch he spotted the JOTUN maid GERDA and fell in love with her. (See "Frey and Gerda," under FREY.)

HNITBORG The mountain stronghold where the giant SUTTUNG hid the Mead of Poetry (see under ODIN), which he had stolen. Suttung's daughter, GUNLOD, stood guard over the vessels containing the MEAD.

HNOSSA (or NOSSA) The daughter of the goddess FREYA and ODUR. Her name means "jewel." The PROSE EDDA tells us that she was so beautiful that her name could be given to whatever is precious or lovely.

HODDMIMIR'S WOOD Another name for the sacred tree YGGDRASIL, used in "The Lay of Vafthrudnir." (see under VAFTHRUDNIR). It was from Hoddmimir's Wood that the two humans, LIF and LIFTHRASIR, emerged at the end of the world, after RAGNAROK.

HODUR, HOD The blind god. His father was ODIN, his mother, FRIGGA, his brother, BALDER. Hodur unwittingly killed Balder with the

HERMOD, ATOP ODIN'S EIGHT-LEGGED STEED, RIDES TO THE UNDERWORLD TO TRY TO RESCUE BALDER FROM THE DEAD.

help of the trickster, LOKI, and a sprig of MIS-TLETOE. He in turn was killed by VALI, the avenger, another son of Odin. After RAGNAROK (the end of the world), Hodur and Balder were reconciled and together returned from HEL to the new world.

HOENIR or HONIR The god of silence. He was one of the three original AESIR gods who, along with his brothers ODIN and LODUR (or VE) created the world. (See "The First Humans," under CREATION.)

After THE WAR BETWEEN THE AESIR AND VANIR, Hoenir went to live with the VANIR as part of an exchange of gods. With him went the wise MIMIR. The Vanir gods became angry when Hoenir appeared to be indecisive and not too quick-witted, always relying on Mimir to make decisions. Because Hoenir was Odin's brother they didn't harm him, but instead they killed Mimir and sent his head back to Odin.

Hoenir is associated with Odin and LOKI in the stories "Idunn's Apples" (see under IDUNN) and "Otter's Ransom" (see under OTTER), when he accompanied the two gods on journeys to earth.

Hoenir survives RAGNAROK, the end of the world. Not much is known about this silent god.

In the POETIC EDDA he is called VILI and his brother Lodur is called VE.

HOFUND The sword of the god HEIMDALL.

HONIR See HOENIR.

HREIDMAR See REIDMAR.

HRAUDING King of the Goths, father of GEIRROD and AGNAR. (See "Geirrod and Agnar," under GEIRROD.)

HRIMFAXI (Frosty Mane) The name of NIGHT's horse from whose bit falls the froth that nightly bedews the earth. (See "Night and Day," under CREATION.)

HRIMGRIMNIR (Rime Mask) The frost giant that will pursue GERDA if she refuses to marry FREY. Also called RIMEGRIM, he is the personi-fication of the cruel cold of northern winters. (See "Frey and Gerda," under FREY.)

HRIMTHURS (Frost Giant) The giant who built the wall around ASGARD. His great stallion, SVADILFARI, helped him in his mighty work. He was killed by THOR. (See "Asgard's Wall and the Giant Builder," under ASGARD.)

HRIMTHURSSAR The frost giants who lived in JOTUNHEIM.

HRUNGNIR Strongest of the giants, he was described as large and stone-headed. He bet his horse GULLFAXI (GOLDEN MANE) in a race with ODIN's eight-legged steed SLEIPNIR. He lost the race, then engaged in a duel with THOR, in which he was killed. (See "Thor's Duel with Hrungnir," under THOR.) SNORRI STURLUSON draws upon HAUSTLANG, a shield poem, for this tale.

HRYM The frost giant who stood at the helm of NAGLFAR, the ship made of dead men's nails, which headed toward the battlefields of RAGNAROK at the end of the world.

HUGI (Thought) The young giant who outran fleet-footed THIALFI, servant of the god THOR, at the court of UTGARD-LOKI. Hugi was, it turned out, the embodiment of THOUGHT, and no one can move faster than thought. (See "Thor's Journey to Utgard," under THOR.)

HUGIN (Thought) One of the god ODIN's two ravens. The other was MUNIN (Memory). The two ravens would fly about the NINE WORLDS, then return to HLIDSKIALF, Odin's high seat, perch on his shoulders and tell him what they had seen.

HUMANS, THE FIRST See "The First Humans," under CREATION.

HVERGELMIR (Roaring Cauldron) The well or spring in NIFLHEIM from which gush the 11 rivers called the ELIVAGAR. The third root of the World Tree, YGGDRASIL, hangs over the poisonous vapor that rises from Hvergelmir. Nearby lives NITHOG, the corpse-eating dragon that nibbles on the roots of the sacred tree.

HYMIR (Dark One) A sea giant who owned a large cauldron that the gods wanted for brewing their ale. The gods TYR and THOR won the cauldron from Hymir and then killed him. (See "Thor and Hymir Go Fishing," under THOR.)

HYNDLA The giantess visited by the goddess FREYA, who asks her to reveal the lineage of her human lover, OTTAR. The story is told in the POETIC EDDA in "THE LAY OF HYNDLA." (See "Freya, Ottar and the Giantess Hyndla," under FREYA.)

"HYNDLULJOTH" A poem; part of the POETIC EDDA. (See "Freya, Ottar and the Giantess Hyndla," under FREYA.)

HYROKKIN The giantess who launched the longship RINGHORN, the funeral pyre of the slain god BALDER. She rode an enormous wolf, using serpents as reins. The BERSERKERS killed the wolf, but Hyrokkin was able to push the ship into the water with her own strength.

I

IDAVOLL The plain or field in ASGARD where the shining palaces of the AESIR gods stood. It was here that the young gods played games such as chess, and it was here that the god BALDER was slain by his blind brother, HODUR. After RAGNAROK (the end of the world), Idavoll became green again at "The Regeneration" (see under RAGNAROK.) New halls were built by the surviving gods. It is said that they found the golden chess pieces of their slaughtered friends and would look at them in wonder as they remembered the past.

IDI One of the storm giants, brother of THIAZZI and GANG, son of OLVALDI, who left piles of gold to be divided among his sons. (See "Skade and Niord," under SKADE.)

IDUNN, IDUNA The flaxen-haired goddess who supplied the AESIR gods with apples that gave them eternal youth. She was the wife of BRAGI, the god of poetry. She was probably an important goddess, but the only myth that survives about Idunn is the one in which she is kidnaped by the giant THIAZZI (see "Idunn's Apples," below).

Idunn's Apples Idunn was the goddess who kept the gods supplied with the apples that kept them forever young. One day Idunn and her apples were stolen away. This is how it happened, as related in SNORRI STURLUSON'S PROSE EDDA.

The great god ODIN, his brother HOENIR and LOKI, the Sly One, went exploring. When they became hungry they killed an ox, built a fire and started to cook the meat. But no matter what they did, the meat remained raw and inedible.

A huge eagle landed on a tree nearby and said that he would make their fire burn like a furnace to cook the meat, if only he could have a share of the food. The hungry travelers agreed to the bargain, the fire burned bright, the meat was cooked and the eagle ate almost all of it in a gulp.

Loki, quick to anger, swiped at the eagle but got carried away in its talons. Loki was dragged over rocks and thorns until he begged for mercy. The eagle wouldn't let Loki go until he promised to deliver to him Idunn and her apples of youth. Loki agreed at once and was dumped back to earth. When he limped back to his companions, he didn't tell them of his promise to the eagle, who he had realized was the giant THIAZZI in disguise.

Back in ASGARD, Loki wasted no time, for he was terrified of the fierce Thiazzi and knew he must somehow keep his promise. He ran to the peaceful orchard that Idunn tended with her husband, BRAGI. He told her that he had found some apples in MIDGARD that looked just like hers. He urged her to bring her basket of apples and accompany him to Midgard, so that they might compare apples.

Sweet Idunn was glad to follow Loki. She would be very happy to find more apples for the gods to eat.

As soon as Idunn and Loki were across BIFROST, the Rainbow Bridge, and into Midgard, the giant eagle swooped down, seized Idunn and carried her away. Once in THRYMHEIM, his fortress, Thiazzi shut the golden maiden in the highest tower.

Without the magic apples, the faces of the AESIR and the ASYNGER—the gods and goddesses—began to wrinkle and sag, their rosy cheeks faded, their hair grew white and thin, their joints stiff and creaky—for these gods and goddesses were billions of years old. The gods and goddesses met to decide what to do. Everyone was there—except Loki. The gods immediately decided that Loki had been up to some mischief. They searched for him and found him.

Odin ordered Loki to bring back Idunn and her apples under threat to his very life.

IDUNN'S MAGIC APPLES PROMISE ETERNAL YOUTH TO THE GODS AND GODDESSES.

Loki fled in terror to the goddess FREYA to borrow her flying suit of falcon feathers. With this he flew off to Thrymheim. Fortunately for Loki, Thiazzi had gone fishing and Idunn was unguarded. Loki used his magic to turn the maiden and her basket of apples into a small nut, which he grasped in his claws.

Odin, the all-seeing, caught sight of the falcon from afar and saw that behind him came an enormous eagle—Thiazzi.

"Quickly build a pile of shavings and kindling at the gates of Asgard," Odin commanded.

Just in time, Loki the Falcon flew over the walls of Asgard. The eagle was so close behind him that he got caught in the flames that roared up when the dry kindling was lighted. He fell to the ground and the gods slew him.

Then Loki said the magic words and Idunn stood before them once more, offering her wonderful apples with a happy smile.

It is interesting to mythologists that Loki turns Idunn into a nut. This symbol of eternal youth is often found in old Scandinavian burial sites. Idunn may have been a Vanir goddess of fertility, youth and death. This is the only surviving myth about her.

In the PROSE EDDA SNORRI STURLUSON bases his retelling of the myth partially on the poem "Haustlong", by mid-9th- to early-10th-century Norwegian poet Thiodor of Hvini.

IRONWOOD The forest east of MIDGARD where lived the wicked witch whose children were werewolves, trolls and the wolves SKOLL and HATI, who would devour the sun and the moon at the last battle, RAGNAROK. (See "Sun and Moon," under CREATION.)

IVALDI Two DWARFS called "the sons of Ivaldi" craft the ship SKIDBLADNIR, ODIN's magic spear, GUNGNIR, and the golden hair for SIF, wife of THOR. (See THE TREASURES OF THE DWARFS.)

J

JACK AND JILL See BIL AND YUKI.

JARNSAXA (Ironstone) One of the wives of the god THOR. She bore him two sons, MAGNI (Strength) and MODI (Courage).

JORMUNGAND The giant serpent, offspring of LOKI and the ogress ANGERBODA; brother of the wolf FENRIS and HEL, the goddess of death. Also known as the Midgard Serpent, MIDGARD SNAKE, or Midgard Worm.

The huge serpent was cast into the sea by ODIN; he was doomed to encircle the earth, his tail in his mouth. He and THOR were mortal enemies. On one occasion Thor catches the serpent using an ox-head for bait, but the giant HYMIR snips the line and the serpent disappears beneath the waves (see "Thor and Hymir Go Fishing," under THOR.) The serpent appears again at RAGNAROK and makes his way onto the land, spewing venom. Thor kills the serpent but is himself poisoned by the deadly venom.

JOTUN The Scandinavian word for "giant." The giants lived in JOTUNHEIM. The first giant was YMIR, formed at the beginning of time out of fire and ice, long before the first gods and men. The first gods, ODIN, VILI and VE, destroyed Ymir and created the world from his body. (See CREATION.) The giants were constantly at war with the gods of ASGARD. At the end of the world, RAGNAROK, gods, giants and monsters would fight a final battle and nearly all would lose.

Giants are generally thought of as personifications of destructive forces, huge, ugly and fierce. They had heads of stone and feet of ice. They were known as frost giants; their names referred to frost (hrim or thrym), storm, snow and ice, scourges of northern winters. They could transform themselves into eagles and wolves. However, in many of the Norse myths they also assume shapes resembling those of normal people (or gods). For example, the builder of Asgard's Wall (see under ASGARD) wasn't at first recognized as a giant. Many of the giantesses were beautiful and more than friendly to the gods. The beautiful GERDA married the god FREY (see "Frey and Gerda," under FREY); the giantess GRID, friend of the great god ODIN, loaned THOR weapons to defend himself against the giant GEIRROD (see "Thor and the Giant Geirrod," under THOR); and HYROKKIN single-handedly pushed Balder's ship, RINGHORN, into the sea at Balder's funeral (see under BALDER). Thor married the giantess JARNSAFA, who bore him two sons, MODI and MAGNI. SKADI, the daughter of the giant THIASSI, married the Vanir god NIORD.

Other giants included Kari (Tempest), BELI (Storm), THRYM (Frost), Johul (Glacier), Frosti (Cold), Snoer (Snow), and Orifta (Snowdrift).

JOTUNHEIM (Giant Land) The mountainous, freezing land of the JOTUN, or giants. Its capital was UTGARD (outer place). It was given to the giants by ODIN after the CREATION.

K

KVASIR (Spittle) A wise man who was created from the spittle of the AESIR and the VANIR gods after their battle. (See WAR BETWEEN THE AESIR AND THE VANIR.) Kvasir walked the world spreading his great wisdom to any who asked for it. He was slain by two DWARFS who mixed his blood with honey to make a powerful MEAD that inspired any who drank it to talk with wisdom and poetry. (See "The Mead of Poetry," under ODIN.)

The word *kvas* or *quaso* means "strong beer" in many parts of eastern Europe and Russia, and "crushed fruit" in Danish. In English a similar word, *squash*, denotes a fruit drink.

In another story Kvasir was a Vanir god noted for his great wisdom. He came to live in ASGARD after the war between the gods, along with the Vanir NIORD, FREY, and FREYA.

L

LAEDING One of the chains with which the gods tried to bind the wolf FENRIS.

LAERAD The great tree around which Odin's hall, VALHALLA, was built. Its leaves were nibbled by the she-goat HEIDRUN, who produced an endless supply of MEAD for the gods and heroes, and also by the stag OAK THORN. Laerad is another name for the World Tree, YGGDRASIL.

LAUFEY (Tree Island) A giantess, the mother of LOKI. Not much is known about her. Some sources say that she gave birth to the mischievous god, Loki, when stricken by a bolt of lightning sent by FARBAUTI, Loki's father.

LAY A short lyric or narrative (story-telling) poem, especially one intended to be sung, usually by traveling minstrels. These minstrels thus kept alive ancient stories dealing with mythology, history or legendary adventures. In Norse mythology many of the poems in the POETIC EDDA are called *lays*.

"LAY OF GRIMNIR" See "GRIMNIRSMAL."

"LAY OF HARBARD" ("Harbardsljoth") See HARBARD.

"LAY OF HYNDLA" A poem, "Hyndluljoth," part of the POETIC EDDA. (See "Freya, Ottar and the Giantess Hyndla," under FREYA.)

"LAY OF THRYM" A poem in the POETIC EDDA that is the only source of "The Theft of Thor's Hammer." (See under THOR.)

"LAY OF VAFTHRUDNIR" See "VAFTHRUDNIR."

LIDSKJALF (High Seat) See HLIDSKIALF.

LIF AND LIFTHRASIR The man, Lif (Life), and the woman, Lifthrasir (Eager for Life), who will survive RAGNAROK and repeople the earth. During the fearful holocaust they take shelter in HODDMIMIR'S WOOD, another name for the World Tree, YGGDRASIL. They are nourished by the morning dew. They emerge from the tree unhurt when they see the new SUN shining. They have children and there is a new beginning for mankind on earth. (From "THE LAY OF VAFTHRUDNIR," see "VAFTHRUDNIR".)

LIFTHRASIR (Eager for Life) The woman, wife of LIF, who survived RAGNAROK and with Lif began to repeople the earth. Lif and Lifthrasir sheltered in the World Tree, YGGDRASIL, during the holocaust that caused the end of the world. (From "The Lay of Vafthrudnir," see "VAFTHRUDNIR.")

LIT The DWARF who suddenly appeared at BALDER'S funeral and got in the way of THOR, who was consecrating the funeral pyre with his magic hammer, MJOLLNIR. Hot-tempered as always and striken with sorrow at Balder's death, Thor kicked Lit into the flames of the pyre. Lit gained immortality in mythology by being burned to ashes along with the god Balder and his wife, NANNA. (See BALDER.)

LITTLE PEOPLE See DWARFS.

LODDFAFNIR A man from MIDGARD, (Middle Earth), that is, a mortal man. In "The Lay of Loddfafnir," part of the poem HAVAMAL from the POETIC EDDA, Loddfafnir tells his fellow men many words of wisdom. He had somehow found his way to the Well of URD, a sacred place, where he heard the words of the High One (ODIN). Loddfafnir recounted these words to fellow mortals. The words contained much good advice: for example, beware of a witch's sweet words; always carry food if you have to cross a mountain; cherish your friends and be loyal to them; stay away from evil people; doing good deeds will make you feel happy; hold to your promises; respect the wisdom of the elderly. There were also words full of ancient superstitions, such as those for warding off the curses made by witches.

"The Lay of Loddfafnir" tells us much about the sound, common-sense values of the ancient Norsemen.

LODUR   See LOTHUR.

LOFNHEID   Daughter of the magician REIDMAR and sister of LYNGHEID, REGIN, FAFNIR and OTTER.

LOGI (Flame)   The young giant who defeated the trickster god, LOKI, in an eating contest at the court of the giant UTGARD-LOKI. It turned out that Logi was the embodiment of fire, which can consume anything and everything with great rapidity. (See "Thor's Journey to Utgard," under THOR.)

"LOKASENNA"   See "Loki's Mocking," under LOKI.

LOKI   Loki is known as the trickster god, the mischief maker, the father of lies and deceit, the shape-changer. He is the personification of both aspects of fire: the merry but potentially dangerous hearth fire and the destructive fire of forest and volcano.

Loki was the son of the giant FARBAUTI and of LAUFEY.

He had two wives. The first was the fearful ogress ANGERBODA, with whom he had three monstrous offspring: HEL, the goddess of death and the underworld; JORMUNGAND, the Midgard Serpent who encircled the world; and FENRIS, the wolf.

His wife in ASGARD was SIGYN, with whom he had two sons, NARVI and VALI.

Loki was counted among the AESIR gods, but he was not one of them, as he was born among the JOTUN, the gods' enemies. Some say that he and the great god ODIN were blood brothers, which is why none of the gods dared to harm Loki, no matter how mischievous and malevolent he became.

Loki was handsome and could be amusing. He made the goddess SKADE laugh even while she mourned for her father, THIAZZI. (See "Skade and Niord," under SKADE.) Loki was sometimes helpful to the gods, for he was quick-witted and always had an answer for everything. But often the gods would regret taking his advice.

It was Loki who accompanied THOR to Jotunland to retrieve Thor's magic hammer. (See "The Theft of Thor's Hammer," under THOR.)

It was Loki who thought of a way to outwit the giant who built Asgard's wall. (See "Asgard's Wall and the Giant Builder," under ASGARD.) However, his solution was nothing but fraud, and resulted in Thor committing murder within Asgard; such behavior was against the code of the Aesir.

Loki stole FREYA's necklace (see "Freya and the Golden Necklace," under FREYA) and cut off SIF's golden hair; but it was he who went down to the underground caves of the DWARFS and brought back wonderful treasures for the gods. (See THE TREASURES OF THE DWARFS.)

Loki double-crossed both the giant Thiazzi and the Aesir when he delivered IDUNN and her apples to the giant and then, disguised as a falcon, carried Idunn back to Asgard, leading Thiazzi to his death. (See "Idunn's Apples," under IDUNN.)

Not only could Loki change himself into other creatures at will, such as a seal, a salmon, a fly, a falcon; he could also change his sex. As a mare, he was the mother of SLEIPNIR, Odin's eight-legged steed. (See "Asgard's Wall and the Giant Builder," under ASGARD.) He became an old crone when he tricked FRIGGA into telling him that MISTLETOE was the only object on earth that could harm the gentle god, BALDER; later he became THOKK, the dour-faced hag who refused to weep for Balder.

Even though Loki was the principal cause of Balder's death, the Aesir took no action against him, though they hated him.

However, when Loki came to AEGIR's banquet (see "Loki's Mocking," below) and flung vicious insults at all the gods and goddesses, the Aesir finally decided to punish the evil creature

LOKI HAD THREE MONSTROUS CHILDREN: FENRIS, THE WOLF, JORMUNGAND, THE MIDGARD SERPENT, AND HEL, QUEEN OF THE UNDERWORLD.

that Loki had become. (See "Loki's Punishment," below.)

At RAGNAROK (the day of doom), Loki led the forces of evil against the gods, and he and HEIMDALL killed each other.

Loki appears as Loge in Richard Wagner's 19th-century opera *The Valkyrie*, where he is asked by Wotan (Odin) to surround BRUNEHILDA by flames.

Loki's Mocking Loki, the trickster god, could be playful and charming. But as time went on, he became sinister, evil and bad-tempered. The story of Loki's mocking of the gods and goddesses shows Loki at his worst.

AEGIR, the JOTUN lord of the sea, invited the gods to a banquet in his coral caves under the island of HLESEY. He brewed the ale in the huge cauldron that THOR and TYR had taken from the giant HYMIR. (See "Thor and Hymir Go Fishing," under THOR.)

It was soon after the death of BALDER and the gods were subdued, talking quietly among themselves. Loki listened impatiently as they praised Aegir's servants, FIMAFENG, the Swift, and ELDIR, the Man of Fire. Suddenly he sprang up and stabbed FIMAFENG with his knife, then fled. But he soon returned, and this time his targets were the gods and goddesses and his weapons were poisonous words.

He insulted BRAGI, the god of poetry, by calling him a soft coward. One by one he accused each of the goddesses, IDUNN, GEFION, FRIGG, FREYA and SIF, of being deceitful and unvirtuous. He laughed at NJORD for being a hostage from the VANIR gods and at Tyr for losing his hand in the jaws of the wolf FENRIS. No one escaped, not even FREY's servants, BARLEY BYGGVIR and his wife BEYLA, nor HEIMDALL, who was mocked as being a mere servant of the gods. Even the great god ODIN didn't escape Loki's evil tongue: Loki sneered at him for once

LOKI MOCKS THE GODS AND GODDESSES WITH POISONOUS WORDS AT AEGIR'S FEAST.

having turned himself into a witch, "a woman through and through."

At last Thor, who had been absent, entered the hall. His eyes glowed with rage and his whiskers bristled when he heard Loki's vicious insults. He threatened to kill Loki there and then with his hammer, and Loki left rather swiftly.

The only source of this myth is "LOKA-SENNA," translated as "Loki's Flyting (or Mocking)," a poem in the POETIC EDDA. It reveals, in Loki's words and in their replies, considerable information about the gods, including the ironic fact that they sink to Loki's level and shout vile things back at him. The poem shows the complete transformation of Loki from mere mischief maker to evil demon.

The Pursuit of Loki-Salmon
Loki, the trickster god, had insulted the gods and goddesses at a feast given by AEGIR, the sea god (see "Loki's Mocking," above).

Loki fled from the wrath of the gods and built himself a hut in the mountains. The hut had doors on all four sides so that Loki could escape easily, for he knew that the gods wanted to punish him for his evil words and also for the death of the gentle god, BALDER.

By day Loki, the Shape-changer, turned himself into a salmon and swam in the mountain torrent at Franang's Falls. To distract himself in the evening, he fashioned a fine net—some say, the first fishing net. (But in other poems the sea ogress RAN, Aegir's wife, invented the fishing net to catch drowning sailors and bring them to her domain under the waves.)

From his high seat, HLIDSKJALF, ODIN could see far and wide over all NINE WORLDS. When he found out where Loki was hiding and in what guise, he went with a party of gods to capture him.

Loki saw them coming and quickly threw the fishing net into the fire, then sprinted down to the stream and leapt in as a salmon.

The gods entered the hut and saw the remains of the net. KVASIR, a very wise god, was able to guess that a finished net might be very useful to the gods for catching slippery Loki-Salmon. The gods sat up all night repairing and completing the net. At dawn they set off to catch Loki.

Loki escaped their clutches for quite a while, as they used the net to drag the stream, but in the end THOR caught him in midair as he made a flying leap out of the stream. To this day, the salmon is noted for its slender tail, a reminder, Northmen say, of how strongly Thor had held Loki in his powerful hand.

Loki's Punishment Loki, the trickster god, had insulted the gods (see "Loki's Mocking," above) and fled from their wrath. But he was captured (see "The Pursuit of Loki," above). In this story we see how the gods punish him.

After the gods had captured Loki, they dragged him into a dark cave. They changed Loki's son VALI into a wolf, who immediately attacked his brother NAVRI, and killed him. The gods took Navri's intestines and bound Loki with them. Once Loki was firmly bound, they changed the horrid bonds into iron.

Now the icy goddess, SKADE, placed a serpent over Loki's upturned face, so that its venom would drip onto him.

Only SIGYN, Loki's faithful wife, stayed with Loki in the miserable cave. She held a bowl to catch the drops of venom. But when she turned aside to empty the poison, the drops fell on Loki's twisted face. He writhed with pain and terror, causing the earth to tremble and quake. So Loki, the Norse myths say, is the cause of the earthquakes that terrify us.

And thus Loki would remain until RAGNA-ROK, when he would wreak his revenge upon the gods and they on him.

LORA or LORRIDE Daughter of THOR and SIF; sister of THRUD.

LORRIDE See LORA.

LOTHUR or LODUR One of the three original AESIR gods who, along with his brothers ODIN

A SERPENT DRIPS VENOM ONTO THE FACE OF LOKI, WHO HAS BEEN BOUND TO A ROCK BY THE GODS.

and HOENIR (or VILI) created the world (see "The First Humans," under CREATION).

Some mythologists have tried to identify Lothur with LOKI, but virtually nothing is known about this god.

In the POETIC EDDA he is called VE and his brother HOENIR is called Vili.

LYNGHEID Daughter of the magician REID-MAR and sister of LOFNHEID, REGIN, FAFNIR and OTTER.

LYNGVI An island in the middle of Lake *Amsvartnir* on which the gods bound FENRIS, the wolf.

M

MAGNI (Mighty) One of the two sons of the god THOR and the giantess JARNSAXA. Brother of MODI. At an early age Magni was strong enough to rescue his father, Thor, from under the leg of the giant HRUNGNIR. As a reward Thor gave him the magnificent horse, GULL-FAXI, which had belonged to the giant. (See "Thor's Duel with Hrungnir," under THOR.) Magni was one of the seven AESIR who survived RAGNAROK, the end of the world, and inherited, with his brother, Modi, Thor's hammer, MJOLLNIR.

MANI The man who drives the chariot that carries the moon across the sky. He is the son of MUNDILFARI and the brother of SOL. For company, Mani stole two children away from MIDGARD (Middle Earth). Their names were BIL (Waning) and YUKI or HJUKI (Waxing). Some say that on a clear night the children in the moon can be seen as dark shapes on the moon's face, as they eternally carry a pail of water on a pole. (See Sun and Moon," under CREATION.) In the end, at RAGNAROK, the moon will be devoured by the wolf HATI, who pursues the chariot across the skies.

MAYPOLE A tree trunk or pole decorated with flowers and streamers. The loose ends were held by dancers who circled around the pole in celebration of spring, usually around the first day of May. This festivity had its origin in pagan remembrances of the world tree, YGGDRASIL, of the Roman goddess Flora and other celebrations of spring in the northern hemisphere.

MEAD An alcoholic drink made by fermenting honey and water. The creators of the Norse myths considered it superior to the usual beer and ale (made by fermenting cereals flavored with hops) drunk by ordinary people. In VALHALLA mead was supplied in a never-ending flow by the she-goat HEIDRUN, and the gods and

ENGLISH VILLAGERS DANCE AROUND THE MAYPOLE ON THE FIRST DAY OF MAY IN THIS ANCIENT ENGRAVING.

heroes would never lack the heavenly brew. (See "The Mead of Poetry," under ODIN.)

MEGINGJARDIR (Also Megingiord, Megingarder) The magic belt of the thunder god, THOR. When he wore it, his already formidable strength was doubled.

MENGLAD (Necklace-Happy) The beautiful maiden who was wooed and won by SVIPDAG.

MIDGARD (Middle Earth) The world of human beings. It was midway between ASGARD, the home of the gods, and JOTUNHEIM, the home of the giants. Midgard was connected to Asgard by BIFROST, the Rainbow Bridge. It was surrounded by an ocean, in which lived JORMUNGAND, the Midgard Serpent. The first man and woman to live in Midgard were ASK and EMBLA. One of the three roots of the sacred tree, YGGDRASIL, was embedded in Midgard. Midgard was formed from the body of the giant YMIR (see CREATION).

MIDGARD SERPENT   See JORMUNGAND.

MIDGARD SNAKE   See JORMUNGAND.

MIDGARD WORM   See JORMUNGAND.

MIDSUMMER EVE   In northern countries, June 21, the longest day, was Balder's Day, celebrated with bonfires and the observance of sunset and sunrise. In many countries it was the custom to gather MISTLETOE on this day. On the Christian calendar June 21 is Saint John's Day. (See BALDER.) Scientifically, it is the day of the summer SOLSTICE.

MIMIR   In one myth Mimir is a wise god sent by the AESIR to the VANIR after the war between the two races of gods (see THE WAR BETWEEN THE AESIR AND THE VANIR). Along with Mimir went HOENIR, who was rather slow-witted. The Vanir were annoyed with Hoenir, and with the Aesir for sending him, but did not dare harm him, for he was ODIN's brother. Instead they cut off Mimir's head and sent it to Odin. Odin used his magic to preserve the head which, ever after imparted its wisdom when Odin came to seek counsel of it.

Another myth tells that Odin sacrificed one of his eyes to Mimir, the guardian of the well of knowledge. Mimir granted Odin permission to drink from the well to gain wisdom and poetic inspiration. (See "Mimir: How Odin Lost His Eye," under ODIN.)

MIMIR'S WELL   The well of wisdom under the second root of the tree YGGDRASIL in JOTUNHEIM. The head of Mimir resides beside the well. The god ODIN visits the well seeking wisdom. HEIMDALL, the watchman of the gods, leaves his horn there until he needs it to announce RAGNAROK, the end of the world. (See "Mimir: How Odin Lost His Eye," under ODIN.)

MISTCALF (Mokkuralfi)   The clay giant made by the JOTUNS as a companion for HRUNGNIR in his duel with the god THOR. Mistcalf was nine leagues tall. (Today we consider a league to be about three miles, but the length has varied in different times and places.) The Jotuns equipped Mistcalf with the heart of a mare. Thor's servant, THIALFI, hacked the clay figure to pieces. (See "Thor's Duel with Hrungnir," under THOR.)

MISTLETOE   A European plant (*Viscum album*) that grows as a parasite on trees. For centuries it was thought of as a mysterious and sacred plant, for it flourishes atop bare-branched trees in the middle of winter, when all other plants seem to be dead. In Norse mythology it is known as the sprig that was hurled at the god BALDER by his blind brother, HODUR. Because mistletoe has weak stems, some scholars suggest that the trickster god, LOKI, used his magic arts on the mistletoe to make it strong and sharp enough to kill Balder. (See BALDER.)

MJOLLNIR   The hammer of the god THOR. It was made by the DWARFS BROKK and SINDRI. The hammer was a symbol of Thor's strength and of the thunderbolt he personified.

The hammer had a massive head and a short

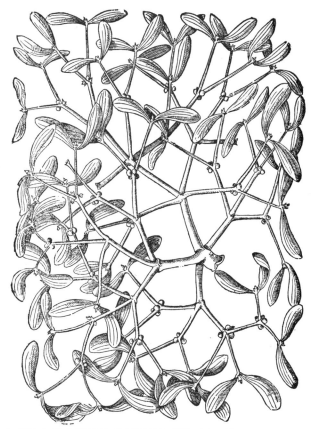

A SPRIG OF MISTLETOE KILLED THE GOD BALDER.

handle and was shaped somewhat like a cross. THE TREASURES OF THE DWARFS tells the reason for its peculiar shape. While Brokk was shaping the hammer in the foundry, he was pestered by the mischievous god, LOKI, who had changed himself into a gadfly. At a crucial point in the making of the hammer, Loki-Fly stung Brokk on his eyelids; the dwarf was distracted and let go of the bellows that he was pumping; thus the shape of the hammer was distorted. For many centuries Northmen wore its likeness as an amulet (a protection, or bringer of good fortune). Many of these amulets have been discovered in Scandinavian and British archaeological digs. Many ancient gravestones and rune stones also depict Thor's hammer.

The gods considered Mjollnir to be their greatest treasure, for it alone could be used to defend ASGARD against the giants. When Thor hurled it, it always struck its mark and returned instantly into his hand, like a boomerang. Although mighty in size, it could be magically shrunk to fit inside Thor's shirt.

The hammer was a symbol of fertility: In "The Theft of Thor's Hammer" (see under THOR), Thor dressed himself as a bride when he went to visit the giant THRYM, who had stolen the hammer. Thor knew that at some point in the wedding ceremony a hammer was always placed in the lap of the bride, for such was the custom of the Northmen.) When this happened, Thor retrieved his hammer.

Mjollnir was also a symbol of resurrection: In "Thor's journey to Utgard" (see under THOR), when Thor waves Mjollnir over the skin and bones of his dead goats, the goats spring back to life.

And Mjollnir was used at funerals: When BALDER lay on his funeral pyre, Thor consecrated the funeral with his hammer.

The hammer was used to kill the giant HRUNGNIR (see "Thor's Duel with Hrungnir," under THOR) and also to kill the giant who built Asgard's wall (see Asgard's Wall and the Giant Builder," under ASGARD).

The only time that the hammer seemed to be ineffectual was when Thor struck the giant SKRYMIR with it. Skrymir said that he thought he was being assaulted by delicate leaves and twigs. However, it turned out that the hammer had made huge dents in a hillside instead of in Skrymir's head, thanks to the giant's clever magic. (See "Thor's Journey to Utgard," under THOR.)

After RAGNAROK, the end of the world, Thor's sons, MAGNI and MODI, inherited Mjollnir.

MODGUD The keeper of the bridge over the Gjall River on the way to HEL. She challenged the god HERMOD, who was searching for his slain brother, BALDER. Modgud told Hermod that Balder was in Hel and told him how to get there.

MODI (Courage) One of the two sons of the god THOR and the giantess JARNSAXA. Along with his brother MAGNI, Modi was one of the seven AESIR gods to survive RAGNAROK. He and Magni inherited Thor's hammer, MJOLLNIR.

MOKKURALFI See MISTCALF.

MOON See "Sun and Moon," under CREATION.

MUNDILFARI (Turner) A man from MIDGARD who named his daughter SOL (Sun) and his son MANI (Moon). The gods were outraged that a human being should have the nerve to call his children after the sun and the moon. They stole the children away and set them to driving the chariots of the sun and the moon eternally through the heavens. (See "Sun and Moon," under CREATION.)

MUNIN (Memory) One of the god ODIN's two ravens. The other was HUGIN (Thought). The two ravens would fly about the NINE WORLDS, then return to HLIDSKIALF, Odin's high seat, perch on his shoulders and tell him what they had seen.

MUSPELLHEIM (Home of Destruction) The realm of fire. Heat from Muspell's fires and ice from NIFLHEIM helped to form the first living beings at the CREATION of the world.

Muspellheim was ruled over by the fire giant, SURT, who guarded it with a flaming sword. At RAGNAROK, the end of the world, Surt burst through a crack in the dome of the sky and destroyed the world by fire. The forces of evil that fought the gods at Ragnarok are called the sons of Musspell.

N

NABBI One of the two DWARFS who fashioned FREYA's gold-bristled boar, HILDISVINI. The other was DAIN.

NAGLFAR (Conveyance Made of Nails) The ship made from dead men's nails. It carried the giants into battle against the gods at RAGNAROK. *Naglfar's* size would depend on how many men had been buried with unpared fingernails; according to ancient superstitions, the nails of the dead must be cut to keep the size of the fatal ship small and thus give the gods a better chance in battle.

NAGLFARI (Darkling) Giant; the first husband of NIGHT or NOTT. Their son was called AUD.

NANNA AESIR goddess, wife of BALDER and mother of FORSETI. After Balder's death Nanna died of grief and was placed on his funeral pyre to burn with him. She accompanied him to HEL and gave gifts to HERMOD for him to take back to ASGARD. Nanna is sometimes referred to as a symbol of vegetation and fertility.

NARFI A giant, the father of NIGHT. Narfi was one of the first giants in JOTUNHEIM. (See "Night and Day," under CREATION.)

NARVI The son of LOKI and SIGYN and the brother of VALI. Narvi is killed by his brother, who has turned into a wolf. His entrails are used to bind Loki to the rocks of an underground cave. (See "Loki's Punishment," under LOKI.)

NASTROND (Strand of Corpses) The gruesome shore in HEL where the corpses of the evil dead are washed up and where the dragon NITHOG feasts. After RAGNAROK (the end of the world) there was still a Nastrond and a Nithog to feed upon the bodies of the dead.

NERTHUS (Earth) Also known as Hertha. A North German goddess, a Mother Earth, worshiped as a goddess of fertility. Some say that she was the sister-wife of the god NIORD and the mother of FREY and FREYA. The Roman historian Tacitus wrote that when Nerthus appeared in her wagon, drawn by oxen, it was a cause for rejoicing throughout the land, and sacrifices were made in her honor.

NIBELUNGELIED (*Song of the Nibelung*) A German poem of the early 13th century. The 19th-century composer Richard Wagner based his music drama, THE RING OF THE NIBELUNG, on the *Nibelunglied,* the VOLSUNGA SAGA and the EDDAS.

NIDAVELLIR (Dark Crags) The home of the DWARFS. Not much is known about the location of Nidavellir in the NINE WORLDS. It may have been an area within SVARTALFHEIM, the home of the dark elves.

NIFLHEIM (World of Fog) A vast waste of frozen fog, brutal cold, and endless night, Niflheim was the lowest region of the underworld. From its poisonous fountain, HVERGELMIR, flowed 11 ice-cold rivers, the ELIVAGIR. The rivers poured into the huge chasm, GINUNNGAGAP, and froze. Fiery clouds from MUSPELLHEIM melted the ice and turned it into mist. From the whirling mist and fire came the first giant, YMIR. (See CREATION.)

Niflheim was the home of the dragon NITHOG and other serpents. They nibbled on one of the roots of the World Tree, YGGDRASIL, that reached into the underworld.

Nearby was HEL, ruled over by the goddess of the dead.

After MIDGARD (the Middle Earth) was created, the gods pushed Niflheim deep into the ground, so that its terrible cold wouldn't freeze the earth.

NIGHT (also called NOTT) The dark-haired daughter of NARFI, one of the first giants of JOTUNHEIM. She married three times. Her first husband was NAGLFARI (Darkling); their son was AUD. Her second husband was ANNAR (Another); their daughter was Earth. Her third husband was DELLING (Dawn); their son was DAY.

The gods gave Night and her son Day each a chariot to ride through the heavens. Night's lead horse was FROSTY MANE. (See "Night and Day," under CREATION.)

NINE WORLDS
In Norse mythology the Nine Worlds were broken into three levels.

- At the top level were ASGARD, the home of the AESIR; VANAHEIM, the home of the VANIR; and ALFHEIM, the home of the light elves.
- At the middle level, and connected to Asgard by BIFROST, the Rainbow Bridge, were MIDGARD (Middle Earth), the home of the first human beings; JOTUNHEIM, the home of the JOTUNS, or giants; and SVARTALFHEIM, home of the dark elves.
- In the underworld were NIFLHEIM, world of the dead, cold and misty, whose citadel was Hel, home of HEL, queen of the dead; and MUSPELLHEIM, world of fire, presided over by the fire god, SURT.

In some tellings of the myths there was also NIDAVELLIR at the middle level; it was cited as the home of the dwarfs and may have been part of Svartalfheim.

The World Tree, YGGDRASIL, connected all Nine Worlds.

From his high seat HLIDSKIALF, the great god ODIN could see what was happening in all Nine Worlds with the help of his ravens.

NIORD (also NJORD)
The Norse god of the sea and seafarers, and also a fertility god. Niord was a VANIR god. He came to live in ASGARD after the WAR BETWEEN THE AESIR AND THE VANIR. He brought with him his twin children, FREY and FREYA, both fertility gods. In some tellings Niord's first wife, and the mother of the twins, was NERTHUS, his sister. As the Aesir did not approve of marriage between brother and sister, Niord had to leave Nerthus behind. His second wife was SKADE, goddess and giantess of winter. Niord's home was NOATUN, a bustling shipyard, noisy with the sound of the wind and the sea and the seabirds. Skade and Niord couldn't live happily together, for Skade hated the cheerful, noisy shipyard, while Niord felt unhappy at Skade's grim, cold mountain home. (See "Skade and Niord," under SKADE.)

NITHOG, NIDHUG (Corpse Tearer)
The dragon that lived in NIFLHEIM at the foot of the World Tree, YGGDRASIL, and gnawed at its roots. The squirrel RATATOSK brought gossipy messages between the eagle at the top of the tree and the evil dragon at the roots. As well as feeding upon the roots of the sacred tree, Nithog fed upon the corpses washed down from NASTROND into the bubbling cauldron of HVERGELMIR. At RAGNAROK, the end of the world, Nithog would harvest many corpses and survive to live in the new world.

NOATUN (Ship Haven)
Hall of the Vanir god NIORD when he came to live in ASGARD. It was on the seashore. Niord, god of seafarers, loved the sound of the waves and the seabirds and the noises of the shipyard, but his wife SKADE did not. (See "Skade and Niord," under SKADE.)

NORDI (North)
One of the four DWARFS that held up the SKY. (See CREATION.)

NORNS, NORNIR (The Fates)
The three spirits of destiny who spun a thread of life for every living being, including gods, men, giants and DWARFS. They shaped the life of each one from the first day to the last.

The three sisters lived near the Well of URD (also called Wyrd) at the foot of the World Tree, YGGDRASIL. Each day they watered the roots of Yggdrasil with the well's sacred water.

The names of the three sisters were URD (Past), VERDANDE (Present), and SKULD (Future). Urd is the oldest of the sisters. Often she is pictured as looking backward to the past. Verdande, the Present, looks straight before her. Skuld, the Future, usually wears a mysterious veil and carries a scroll in her hands.

The three sisters were even more powerful than the gods, for the thread they spun was the destiny of the universe. They measured time and controlled it, and the gods were helpless

THE NORNS (PAST, PRESENT AND FUTURE) SPIN THE WEBS OF FATE FOR ALL CREATURES.

against them. The gods held all their important meetings by the Well of Urd, which was a sacred place to them.

In northern folklore the Norns sometimes appear as fairy godmothers or spinners (for example, in the tale "The Sleeping Beauty.") The SPIDER, a spinner, is associated with the Norns. The Norns appear in Richard Wagner's opera, *Gotterdammerung,* ("The Twilight of the Gods"). The three sisters in Shakespeare's trag-edy *Macbeth* are related to the Norns of ancient lore. The Norns are mentioned in both the PROSE EDDA and the POETIC EDDA.

Belief in the Norns or Fates persisted long after the advent of Christianity.

See also FYLGIE.

NOSSA See HNOSSA.

NOTT See NIGHT.

O

OAK The largest tree of the forests that covered northern Europe, it was the one most often struck by lightning. It seemed to serve as a direct pathway from heaven to earth and was sacred to THOR, god of thunder and lightning, and a symbol of strength and endurance. There were no great oaks in Iceland, but early settlers from the Norse lands brought oak pillars with them and set up shrines to Thor. Early Christian missionaries such as Boniface (8th century) considered it their duty to destroy oak trees and groves where the pagan gods had been worshiped. The ancient custom of raising a branch or a small sapling on the roof once a building is completed may date back to our ancestors' superstition that a branch of sacred oak on, in or near a house would protect it from thunder and lightning.

OAK THORN The stag who nibbles the leaves of the tree LAERAD in VALHALLA. From his horns a stream drips into HVERGELMIR, the roaring cauldron from which runs every river in the NINE WORLDS.

OD, ODUR The husband of FREYA and father of HNOSSA. Odur left Freya to roam the earth; it is said that Freya wept golden tears for her lost husband. Some scholars think that Odur may have been the god ODIN in one of his many guises.

ODIN Chief of the AESIR gods; the god of war and death; a sky god and the god of wisdom and poetry. He is sometimes called All-Father, the father of the gods.

He was descended from one of the earliest gods, BOR, and the giantess BESTLA. His brothers were VILI and VE (also called HOENIR and LOTHUR). (See CREATION.)

Odin's Aesir wife was FRIGGA. His sons included THOR, VALI and possibly TYR. Odin had many other wives and children.

Odin's hall in ASGARD was VALASKJALF. From the throne in its high tower, HLIDSKIALF, Odin could survey all the NINE WORLDS.

His ravens HUGIN and MUNIN (Thought and Memory) brought Odin news. He gave his food to his two wolves GERI and FREKI (Greedy and Fierce), for Odin needed nothing but the sacred MEAD for nourishment.

Odin's eight-legged steed was called SLEIPNIR; his spear was GUNGNIR.

On his arm Odin wore the marvelous ring DRAUPNIR, from which dropped eight other rings every nine nights.

When he rode into battle Odin wore an eagle helmet and armor. When he wandered peacefully on earth (as he often did), Odin wore a sky-blue cape and a broad-brimmed hat.

Odin had only one eye, for he had given his other eye to MIMIR in exchange for wisdom. (See "Mimir: How Odin Lost His Eye," below.) Odin was the wisest of the gods.

Odin was also thought of as a magician, for he knew the secrets of the RUNES (the earliest alphabet used by the Norsemen), which he had obtained by hanging himself for nine days and nine nights from the sacred World Tree, YGGDRASIL. He is sometimes called "Lord of the Gallows" (see below). It is said that he sends his ravens or goes himself to visit hanged men, in memory of his ordeal.

In addition Odin could compose poetry, for he had drunk "The Mead of Poetry" (see below).

Odin had another palace called VALHALLA, where he entertained heroes who had fallen in battle and who would help him fight the frost giants at RAGNAROK, the end of the world. But Odin and most of his warriors would be killed at Ragnarok, Odin by the monster-wolf, FENRIS.

Many wonderful tales are told about Odin, the greatest of the gods. He had as many as 200 different names and attributes. (See "Odin's Names," below.)

Odin, along with THOR, FREY and TYR, was

THIS CARVED STONE FROM GOTLAND, SWEDEN, SHOWS ODIN ON HIS EIGHT-LEGGED STEED, SLEIPNIR, AND (*BELOW*) WARRIORS ABOARD A VIKING LONGSHIP.

worshiped for many years after the coming of Christianity to northern Europe (see "Odin Worship," below).

The fourth day of the week, WEDNESDAY, is named for Odin; Woden was one version of Odin's name.

In Richard Wagner's music drama, THE RING OF THE NIBELUNG, Odin is called Wotan.

Lord of the Gallows ODIN was called Lord of the Gallows, God of the Hanged and God of the Spear, among many other names. Odin was the god of knowledge. He paid dearly for his wisdom. In one myth (HAVAMAL, or WORDS OF THE HIGH ONE), he hanged himself from the branches of YGGDRASIL, the sacred tree. He wounded himself with his spear and hung on the tree for nine days and nine nights, without food or water. At the end of that time he came back to life and picked up the magic RUNES that had dropped from the tree. The runes brought secret knowledge to Odin. He passed on this wisdom to both gods and men.

In later years men would make human sacrifices to Odin by hanging them on gallows. It was said that Odin and his ravens would visit the victims and talk to them.

Odin underwent other hardships in his quest for knowledge. See "Odin's Visit to the Vala," under BALDER, and "Mimir: How Odin Lost His Eye" (below).

The Mead of Poetry The Mead of Poetry was the wondrous liquid created by the gods after the WAR BETWEEN THE AESIR AND THE VANIR. Whoever drank the MEAD would acquire wisdom and the inspiration to make poetry.

After the truce between the two races of gods (the AESIR and the VANIR), each god and goddess spat into a great jar to put a seal on their friendship. According to one myth, the Aesir then carried off the jar and out of the spittle they fashioned a man, KVASIR, who walked the world spreading great wisdom to all who asked for it.

Kvasir was slain by the wicked DWARFS FJALAR and GALAR, who collected his blood in three vats and mixed it with honey to make a powerful mead, which they would share with no one. One day, in a fit of rage, the dwarfs murdered the giant GILLING and his wife. They were forced to give the mead to Gilling's angry son, SUTTUNG, in exchange for their lives.

Suttung built a strong underground cave in the mountain HNITBORG, where he lived. There he placed the three containers of mead, and entrusted his daughter, GUNLOD, to guard them.

Because Suttung was a boastful, bragging kind of giant, it wasn't long before the Aesir heard what had happened to the divine mead.

ODIN, a master of disguise, turned himself into a giant of a man, and went to JOTUNHEIM, calling himself BOLVERK. There, he sharpened the scythes of nine slaves who were at work in the fields owned by the giant BAUGI, Suttung's brother. The slaves managed to kill each other with their carefully honed scythes.

As Baugi now had no fieldhands, he agreed to let Bolverk-Odin work for him, for the one-eyed man looked very strong and seemed to need no rest. Odin put his magic to use. He worked better than nine men, for Baugi had promised to try to persuade his brother to allow Bolverk a sip of the famous mead as a reward for his work.

When the work was done, Baugi did talk to his brother, but of course Suttung refused to part with even one drop of mead. Baugi then drilled a hole into the mountain with the auger RATI, and Bolverk-Odin quickly turned himself into a slender serpent and squirmed his way into the chamber where Gunlod guarded the treasure.

When lonely Gunlod saw Odin, once more in the shape of a tall, handsome man, she forgot all the promises she had made to her father, and entertained Odin for three days and three nights. At the end, she even offered Odin a sip of the precious mead from each of the three containers, SON, BODN and ODRORIR. To her dismay, Odin gulped down the entire contents of the vats, turned himself into an eagle and flew off to Asgard. He was closely pursued by Suttung, who had tasted the mead and so knew some magic and could change his shape to that of a powerful eagle. But the gods had lighted a great fire just outside the walls of Asgard. Suttung fell into this and was burned to death.

Odin spat the precious mead into the vessels that the gods eagerly held out. But in his haste to escape Suttung, he spilled some of the mead, which fell to earth (MIDGARD). That is how some lucky people on earth acquired the gift of poetry.

The source for this myth is in the PROSE EDDA; and *Havamal* in the POETIC EDDA.

Mimir: How Odin Lost His Eye MIMIR was an ancient being noted for his wisdom. According to one myth, Mimir was the guardian of a sacred well (MIMIR'S WELL) that gave knowledge to those that drank of it. Odin so coveted wisdom that he gave up one of his eyes to Mimir to gain the privilege of drinking from the well. Mimir placed the eye in the well, where it shone as brilliantly as the moon.

Odin's Names Odin had more than 200 names and attributes. Here are some of them:
Alfodr (All-Father), Father of the Gods
Atridr, Rider Through the Skies
Baleygr, Flaming Eyed
Bileygr, Shifty Eyed
Bolverk (Worker of Misfortune) (see "The Mead of Poetry," above)
Farmatyr, God of Cargoes
Fjolsvidr, Wide in Wisdom
Glapsvidir, Swift in Deceit
Grim or Grimnir, Hooded One (see GRIM)
Oski, Wish Giver
Sidfodr, Father of Victories
Svipall, Changing
Valfodr, Father of the Slain
Veratyr, Lord of Men
Voden, Woden, Wotan, Wuotan—variant forms of Odin
Ygg, Awful

ODRORIR A cauldron. One of the three containers into which the DWARFS poured "The Mead of Poetry" (see under ODIN). The other containers were called BODN and SON.

OLVALDI JOTUN father of storm giants THIAZZI, IDI and GANG. Olvaldi left such a large amount of gold to his sons that no scales could weigh it, so the sons measured it out in giant mouthfuls after their father's death. (See "Skade and Niord," under SKADE.)

OTTAR The human lover of the goddess FREYA. He builds an altar to Freya and offers sacrifices. Freya helps him to win a bet by turning him into her boar, HILDISVINI, and taking him to visit the giantess and seeress HYNDLA. Hyndla reveals that Ottar is the son of Instein and the priestess Hledis and that SIGURD, the greatest of Germanic heroes, is among his ancestors. (See "Freya, Ottar and the Giantess Hyndla," under FREYA.)

OTTER Son of REIDMAR and brother of REGIN and FAFNIR. Otter was a shape-changer and usually took the form of an otter. He was killed by the trickster god, Loki. Reidmar demanded as ransom enough gold to cover the dead otter's pelt and to fill its insides. (See "Otter's Ransom," below.)

Otter's Ransom Otter was the son of the magician REIDMAR. Something of a magician himself, Otter often took the form of an otter. One day ODIN, his brother HOENIR and his blood-brother LOKI were walking by a stream in MIDGARD. They saw an otter. Loki threw a stone at it and killed it. Then he picked up the otter and flung it over his shoulders.

The three came to the prosperous farmhouse of Reidmar and asked for shelter for the night. At first Reidmar was welcoming enough, but when he saw the otter he shouted in rage and grief, for the dead creature was his son.

He summoned his other two sons, REGIN and FAFNIR. Then, with his magic spells, he disarmed the gods and bound them. Now the gods recognized Reidmar as the master magician of the trolls and DWARFS. He was very powerful indeed.

Odin told Reidmar that he and his companions would pay whatever ransom he asked, for they had slain his son—but unknowingly, thinking that the creature was a real otter. Justice demanded that Reidmar should be paid for his misfortune, but there was no need to start a blood feud.

Calmed by Odin's fairness, Reidmar and his sons demanded that the otter's skin should be stuffed with gold inside and the outside covered with gold until not a whisker could be seen.

Odin and Hoenir agreed among themselves

that, sly and cunning as he was, Loki would be the best one to go out and find enough gold for the awesome task, for the otter skin was growing bigger by the minute.

Freed of his bonds, Loki went straight to the place where he had killed the otter and stared down into the water. Soon he saw what he was looking for—an enormous pike guarding the entrance to an underwater cave that gleamed with gold. The pike was the dwarf ANDVARI, keeper of the fabled treasure.

Quickly Loki sped to the island of HLESEY where RAN, the ogress of the oceans, lived with her husband AEGIR, god of the sea. Loki borrowed from her the cruel net with which she dragged drowning sailors to her underwater realm. With the killing net, Loki had no difficulty in scooping up the pike. He landed it on the bank where it lay gasping and gradually changed into the ungainly shape of the dwarf.

To save his life, Andvari gave up his entire hoard of gold, all but a single ring. This he begged Loki not to take from him.

But Loki snatched up the ring and put it on his finger. Andvari laid a terrible curse upon the ring, vowing that anyone who wore it would be smitten with ill fortune and death.

The eyes of Reidmar and his sons glittered greedily when they saw the gold. Odin, Hoenir and Loki stuffed the otter's pelt and then made a blanket of gold all around the outside of it. Reidmar examined it critically then pointed out a whisker that was exposed. Odin had seen Andvari's ring on Loki's finger. Loki pulled it off and laid it upon the whisker.

Thus was Otter's ransom paid and the three travelers allowed to go—but not without a parting shot from Loki. He told Reidmar that he and his sons were doomed to ill fortune and death, for that was the curse of Andvari.

This myth from the PROSE EDDA forms a preface to the SIGURD legends, in which Reidmar is murdered by his sons, Regin and Fafnir. Fafnir then steals the dwarf's treasure for himself and turns himself into a frightful dragon, the better to guard it. In the end the dragon is slain by the hero, Sigurd.

The myth "Otter's Ransom" is told by SNORRI STURLUSON in the *Prose Edda;* it is mentioned in the 13th-century *Codex Regius* (POETIC EDDA) and in the late 13th-century VOLSUNGA SAGA. All these tellings relate "Otter's Ransom" to the legend of Sigurd, the greatest of Germanic heroes, using the story of Otter as a preface to the tales of Sigurd's exploits.

P

POETIC EDDA A collection of poems on mythological and legendary themes, written down from the oral tradition by many different poets at different times, between the 8th and the 13th centuries. The *Poetic Edda* is sometimes called the *Elder Edda* because most of its material predates the 13th-century PROSE EDDA by SNORRI STURLUSON. The *Poetic Edda* consists of the following:

- *The Codex Regius*, which contains some 30 mythical and heroic poems, probably written about 1270, and discovered by Icelandic Bishop Sveinsson in 1643. (It was erroneously called "Saemund's Edda" in old references, after the Icelandic Bishop Saemund, who was once thought to have written the poems.)
- *The Arnamagnean Codex*, another, smaller group of poems, including "Balder's Dreams" (see under BALDER);
- The "VOLUSPA," an account of the origins of the world, its present state, its destruction at RAGNAROK, and the new world. Many scholars believe that "Voluspa" is one of the greatest achievements of the Germanic world.

Other poems of the *Poetic Edda* include:

- "Alvismal" ("The Lay of Alvis") See ALVIS.
- *Flateyjarbok* ("Book of the Flat Island," source of the myth "HYNDLA")
- "Grimnismal" ("The Lay of Grimnir") See "Geirrod and Agnar," under GEIRROD.
- "Harbarthsjoth" ("The Lay of Harbard") See HARBARD.
- *Havamal* (*Words of the High One*) See LODDFAFNIR.
- "Hymiskvitha" ("The Lay of Hymir") See "Thor and Hymir Go Fishing," under THOR.
- "Hyndluljoth" ("The Lay of Hyndla") See "Freya, Ottar and the Giantess Hyndla," under FREYA.

- *"Lokasenna"* ("Loki's Mocking") See "Loki's Mocking," under LOKI.
- "Reginsmal" ("The Lay of Regin") See "Otter's Ransom."
- "Rigsthula" ("The Lay of Rig") See "Rig Heimdall and the Races of Man," under HEIMDALL.
- "Skirnismal" ("The Lay of Skirnir") See "Frey and Gerda," under FREY.
- "Svipdagsmal" ("The Lay of Svipdag") See SVIPDAG.
- "Thrymsvitha" ("The Lay of Thrym") See "The Theft of Thor's Hammer," under THOR.
- "Vafthrudnismal" ("The Lay of Vafthrudnir") See VAFTHRUDNIR.

Other poems in the *Poetic Edda* deal with mortal heroes (rather than gods) of the Northlands, for example SIGURD.

PROSE EDDA A handbook for poets and scholars written by Icelandic poet, historian and diplomat SNORRI STURLUSON (1179–1241), around 1220. It is a handbook of Norse mythology, designed as a guide for poets to encourage them to write in the style of the ancient poets of the Viking Age. Because it was written later than the POETIC EDDA (8th–13th centuries), it was known as the *Younger Edda* and sometimes as the *Snorra Edda*.

The *Prose Edda* consists mostly of:

- "Gylfaginning" *(The Beguiling of Gylfi)*, which tells the myths of the Norse gods. It is an important source for some of the tales (see GEFION and GYLFI).
- SKALDSKAPARMAL *(Poetic Diction)*, a listing of the condensed metaphors, called kennings, frequently used in Viking poetry. Two examples of kennings are "Sif's hair" for "gold" (see THE TREASURES OF THE DWARFS), and "Kvasir's blood" for "poetry" (see "The Mead of Poetry," under ODIN). The *Skald* also has some mythological and legendary tales.

- "Hattatal" *(The Meters of Poetry)* A poem by Snorri Sturluson about King Haakon and Duke Skuli of Norway during the years 1221 and 1223.

For mythologists, the major interest of the *Prose Edda* is in "Gylfaginning," which deals with the Norse myths of the gods and giants.

Snorri Sturluson wrote this guide to old Icelandic poetry and mythology in the 13th century, when Christianity was well established in Iceland and knowledge about the old gods and their adventures was dying out. He wanted to preserve the ancient knowledge. Snorri was a wonderful storyteller: He recounted the old stories with zest, humor and tolerance. Sometimes he quotes from sources that are still available to us; at other times he quotes from poems and stories that are now lost forever. The *Prose Edda* has become a handbook for all writers and scholars who want to keep alive the ancient myths of the Norsemen.

R

RAGNAROK (the Doom of the Gods) The final battle between the gods, headed by ODIN and the EINHERIAR on the side of good, and LOKI and the frost giants on the side of evil. It takes place on the plain called VIGRID. Nearly all the participants are slain; the sun and the moon are swallowed by wolves, the stars vanish, the sacred tree YGGDRASIL trembles, the ocean boils, and SURT (the fire god) sets the world on fire so that everything is reduced to cinders. However, BALDER and HODUR rise up from HEL; VALI and VIDAR, and MODI and MAGNI, and some others survive to live in a regenerated world. A human couple, LIF and LIFTHRASIR, also survive and repeople the earth.

Richard Wagner's *Gotterdämmerung (The Twilight of the Gods)*, the final opera in the "Ring" cycle, dramatically portrays the destruction of the gods.

Ragnarok is dealt with in the Icelandic poem "VOLUSPA" ("The Sibyl's Prophecy"), and in the PROSE EDDA.

(See "Ragnarok, The Day of Doom," below.)

Ragnarok, The Day of Doom The end of the world, the twilight of the gods. Ragnarok was the final battle between the forces of good (the gods) and the forces of evil (the giants and the monsters of the underworld). After the death of BALDER, the gods banished LOKI, the evil one, to MIDGARD (Middle Earth), but it was too late. The god of light and innocence had been killed. The gods knew that Ragnarok, the day of doom, was at hand and that they and all their worlds would perish. And so it was.

First came a wave of ghastly crimes and bloody wars in Midgard; brothers fought against brothers; there was murder and looting and other evil deeds. Then came FIMBUL WINTER, the worst of all winters. It brought bitter cold and driving snow, screeching winds and black darkness. The Fimbul Winter lasted for three years. People shivered and starved and lost all hope and goodness.

From IRONWOOD came the ravening wolves SKOLL and HATI. Skoll caught up with SOL's chariot at last and swallowed the sun, spilling her blood on the earth. Hati devoured the moon. The stars fell out of the sky and the darkness was complete.

Then the earth began to tremble and quake, and the wolf FENRIS broke from his bonds, ready to seek vengeance on the gods who had tricked him. Loki, too, broke free. GARM, the Hel Hound, was free. Evil and destruction were loose on the land.

EGGTHER, the watchman of the giants, struck a note on his harp. The red cock FJALAR crowed to the giants, while GULLINKAMBI screeched to the gods in VALHALLA and a third rooster, rust red, awakened all the dead in NIFLHEIM.

HEIMDALL, the watchman of the gods, lifted his horn, GIALLAR, and blew it. All the AESIR and the EINHERIAR sprang up and donned their armor, ready for the battle to end all battles. But first ODIN galloped off on SLEIPNIR to MIMIR's Well to seek his wisdom. The NORNS regarded him with veiled faces, their web of life rent into shreds. No one knew what Odin learned from Mimir, the Wise. He rejoined the waiting army with a grim, sad face, and led them into battle, holding aloft his magic spear, GUNGNIR.

Now the sea began to boil like a cauldron and its waves crashed on the shore, for JORMUNGAND, the Midgard Serpent, had risen up from the deep and was lashing and writhing his way toward the land, spewing venom from his jaws.

The horrid ship NAGLFAR, made from dead men's nails, drifted loose, packed with giants and steered by HRYM. It headed toward the battlefield, which was called VIGRID. The crew and passengers of Loki's ship were all the pale dead from Hel.

HEL, the goddess of death, left Niflheim to join the fray, followed by the hound, Garm, and the dragon, NITHOG, who flew over the battlefield gathering corpses for his sustenance.

AT RAGNAROK, THOR ATTACKS THE MIDGARD SERPENT WITH HIS HAMMER WHILE ODIN DOES BATTLE WITH FENRIS, THE WOLF.

Loki led the terrible army of evil. As they crossed the Rainbow Bridge, BIFROST, it trembled and broke beneath them, but not before they had reached Vigrid.

Odin, the mighty leader of the gods, was the first to attack. He joined battle with the monster-wolf, FENRIS, whose slavering jaws grew wider and wider, stretching from heaven to earth, until they swallowed up Odin.

Nearby THOR, the god of thunder, wrestled with Jormungand. In the deathly struggle the serpent was vanquished, but Thor, too, died a gasping death from the beast's fatal venom.

Loki and Heimdall, lifelong enemies, killed each other.

FREY, the god of fertility, grappled with the fire god, SURT, in a lengthy battle. Frey had given away his magic sword long ago for love of GERDA, and now, without it, he was killed by the fire demon.

TYR, who had only one hand, fought bravely with GARM, and the two killed each other.

All around the battle raged, and all were doomed to perish. But VIDAR, son of Odin, avenged his father. On his foot he wore a boot made from all the strips of leather snipped off and saved by good cobblers for just this purpose. Vidar crushed his magic boot onto the lower jaw of Fenris, and, using all his strength, he tore the wolf apart.

Now that Odin and most of the other gods, heroes, giants and monsters were dead, Surt (who some say was Loki in another shape) flung his brands of fire all over the earth, so that there was a great and terrible conflagration. All NINE WORLDS went up in flames, and at last the earth

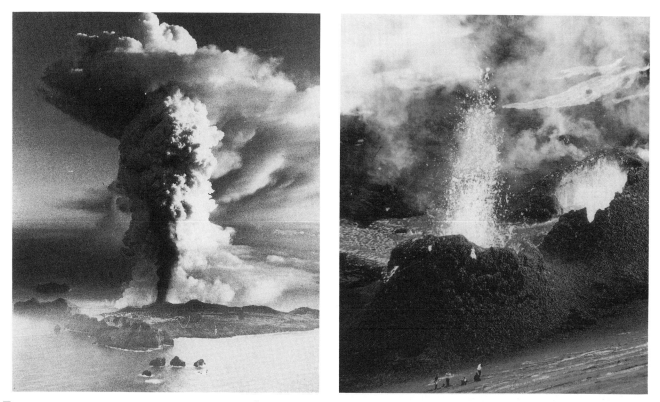

THESE PICTURES OF ERUPTING VOLCANOES IN ICELAND SHOW THAT EDDIC DESCRIPTIONS OF RAGNAROK WERE SURELY BASED ON THE POETS' OWN EXPERIENCES OF FIRE AND CALAMITY IN THEIR NATIVE LAND.

sank into the boiling sea.

The idea of Ragnarok (the end of the world followed by its rebirth) is similar to Christian and Oriental conceptions of Doomsday or Judgment Day. However, the dramatic descriptions of darkness, earthquakes, flood, fire and ashes undoubtedly came straight from the Icelandic poets' own experiences of volcanic eruptions in their native land.

The Regeneration After the terrible destruction of RAGNAROK, the end of the world, all was not lost, after all, for there was a rebirth: Two human beings emerged, some of the gods survived, green plants grew and a new world was born.

Before she had been devoured by the wolf, SOL had given birth to a daughter, as brilliant and burning as she. And as that new sun appeared, darkness vanished, and a new day dawned in a world that gradually, magically, became green and pleasant, with fields of corn growing where no seeds had been planted.

From the remains of the sacred tree, YGG-DRASIL, stepped a human man, LIF, and a woman, LIFTHRASIR. They had been nourished by dew and were unhurt by SURT's fire. They would repeople the earth.

VIDAR and VALI survived, so did MODI and MAGNI, THOR's sons, who had inherited his hammer, MJOLLNIR. Balder came back from the dead, leading his blind brother, HODUR. HOENIR appeared, and so did VILI and VE, Odin's brothers. They went to IDAVOLL, which had remained unscorched, and there they built new mansions, the greatest of which was GIMLÉ, roofed with gold. Another was BRIMIR, on the place called OKOLNIR ("Never cold"). SINDRI rose up in the mountains of NIDAFJOLL. All these places were good. But there was also a hall on NASTROND, the shore of corpses. All its doors faced north to greet the shrieking winds; the walls were made of writhing snakes who poured their venom into a river that flowed through the hall. This was the new underworld, full of murderers and thieves, and when they died, NITHOG, who had survived, was there to feed upon the corpses.

AT THE REGENERATION AFTER RAGNAROK NEW PLANTS SPROUTED WHERE NOTHING HAD BEEN SOWN AND THE WORLD BECAME GREEN AGAIN.

The AESIR walked on the new green grass of Idavoll and talked quietly about the past and their dear, perished friends. They played chess with the golden pieces that they found on the ground, and they thought with wonder about the new life of the earth.

RAINBOW An arc of colored light seen in the sky opposite to the sun. It is caused by the sun's rays being seen through drops of water in the sky. The light is broken up into seven colors: red, orange, yellow, green, blue, indigo and violet. This ethereally beautiful arc across the sky has always been held in awe by people all over the world, for it is a universal happening of nature. In the Judeo-Christian tradition it symbolizes God's promise to show mercy to mankind (Genesis 9:12–15). The Greeks and Romans saw it as a sign from Iris, the messenger of the gods. Fairytales tell that a pot of gold is hidden at the foot of the rainbow. The rainbow in Norse mythology was BIFROST, the three-stranded bridge that stretched between ASGARD and MIDGARD, that is, between the gods of heaven and the ordinary mortals of earth.

RAINBOW BRIDGE See BIFROST.

RAN (Robber) The wife of AEGIR, JOTUN lord of the sea. She lived with Aegir beneath the island of HLESEY, in coral caves. She dragged drowning sailors down to her realm in her fishing net, which either she or LOKI invented. Her halls were lighted only by the gleam of gold, reminiscent of the phosphorescent glow of the sea. It is said that she felt kindly toward dead sailors who had some gold in their possession to help her light her halls. In "Otter's Ransom," (under OTTER), Loki borrows Ran's drowning net to catch the DWARF ANDVARI; in "The Pursuit of Loki-Salmon" (under LOKI), Loki himself is trapped in a net.

RAPID GOER (Alsvider) The horse that pulled the sun's chariot across the sky for MANI. (See "Sun and Moon," under CREATION.)

RATATOSK The squirrel who scampered up and down the World Tree, YGGDRASIL. He spread gossip and carried insults between NITHOG, the dragon who nibbled at the roots of the tree, and the eagle who sat in the topmost branches.

RATI The name of the auger used by the giant BAUGI to drill a hole into the mountain HNITBORG. (See "The Mead of Poetry," under ODIN.)

REGENERATION See under RAGNAROK.

REGIN Son of the magician REIDMAR and brother of FAFNIR and OTTER. After Fafnir killed Reidmar and stole his treasure (see "Otter's Ransom," under OTTER), Regin adopted the young hero, SIGURD, and ordered him to kill Fafnir, who had turned himself into a dragon. Regin was later killed by Sigurd.

REIDMAR (or HREIDMAR) A master magician. Father of REGIN, FAFNIR and OTTER. Otter was killed by the trickster god, LOKI. As compensation for his son's death, Reidmar was given the DWARF ANDVARI's treasure of gold. (See "Otter's Ransom," under OTTER.) Reidmar was killed by Fafnir, who stole the treasure and turned himself into a dragon.

RIG The name taken by the god HEIMDALL when he went to MIDGARD (Middle Earth) and helped to found the races of men. The story is told in "Rigsthula," an ancient poem found in the POETIC EDDA. (See "Rig-Heimdall and the Races of Men," under HEIMDALL).

"RIGSTHULA" An ancient poem found in the POETIC EDDA. It tells how the god HEIMDALL helped to found the races of men. (See "Rig-Heimdall and the Races of Men," under HEIMDALL.)

RIMEGRIM (Rime Mask) See HRIMGRIMNIR.

RINDA (Rind) Daughter of King Billing of the Ruthenians, mate of the god ODIN, mother of VALI. She appears only once in the myths, as the temporary wife of Odin. Rinda is a personification of the hard-frozen rind of the earth, who at first resists the wooing of Odin (the sun) but finally succumbs to his warmth and gives birth to Vali, the light god of spring. (See "Vali, The Avenger," under VALI.)

RINGHORN The longship of the god BALDER. It was perhaps named for the intricate, curving ring designs with which it (and many Norse ships) was adorned. When Balder was slain, the funeral pyre for his body was built on *Ringhorn.* The fire was set ablaze by THOR and the ship was sent out to sea. As it disappeared over the horizon, it must have looked like the setting sun and people mourned for the god of light, now darkened. (See SHIPS AND SHIP BURIALS.)

THE RING OF THE NIBELUNG Four epic music-dramas by German composer Richard Wagner; first performed in 1876. The stories are based on the *"Nibelungelied"* ("Song of the Nibelung"), written by a German poet of the early 13th century. *The Ring* also borrows from the VOLSUNGA SAGA and the EDDAS. It is an interesting and dramatic interpretation of some of the Norse myths, as well as being an innovative and stirring form of opera.

Wagner's *Ring* consists of four operas: *The Rhinegold,* which bears a close resemblance to the myth "Otter's Ransom, (see under OTTER); *The Valkyrie,* where the heroine is BRUNHILDA, a daughter of ODIN, here called Wotan. The plot contains elements from the myth "Asgard's Wall and the Giant Builder," (see under ASGARD); *Siegfried,* hero of the *Volsunga Saga;* and *The Twilight of the Gods,* in which VALHALLA is consumed in flames in a scene reminiscent of the Norse RAGNAROK.

ROSKVA The farmer's daughter who becomes the god THOR's servant, along with her brother THIALFI. Thor took the brother and sister to be his eternal servants after Thialfi had disobeyed his command not to mutilate the bones of his goats. (See "Thor's Visit to Utgard," under THOR.)

ROSTIOFF In some tellings of the myths, Rostioff is the wizard who prophesied that from the union of ODIN and RINDA a son, VALI, would be born and that Vali would avenge the death of BALDER. The wizard lived in Lappland. (See "Vali, The Avenger," under VALI.)

ROWAN (Mountain Ash) A tree of the rose family, not related to the common ash tree. A sturdy tree, it has dense white blossoms and clusters of red fruit well loved by birds. Old superstitions say that the tree has protective qualities, especially against witches (it is sometimes called witch-wood or witchen tree). In Scotland to this day it is often planted near the front door of a house. In Norse mythology it is called "Thor's Salvation" or "Thor's Tree of Deliverance," because it saved THOR from drowning in the river VIMUR. (See "Thor and the Giant Geirrod," under THOR.)

RUNES ("that which is secret") Ancient letters or symbols used in the earliest alphabets of the German tribes of northern Europe from the 2nd to the 12th centuries A.D. Runic inscriptions occur most commonly in Scandinavia and parts of the British Isles. They may have been adapted from characters in the Greek alphabet.

Magical and mysterious powers were associated with runes. The characters consisted of perpendicular, slanting and curved lines, well adapted to being carved on wood, stone and metal.

After the establishment of Christianity, runes were looked down upon as pagan, though in Scandinavia their use continued after the Middle Ages in manuscripts as well as in inscriptions on stone, metal and wood.

In Norse mythology, knowledge of runes was introduced by the god ODIN, who hanged himself from the branches of the sacred tree, YGG-DRASIL, for nine days and nine nights until fallen twigs from the tree spelled out the secret of the runes. Because runes were a form of writing, people now had a way to share their thoughts with others far away or as-yet unborn. (See "Lord of the Gallows," under ODIN.)

English Runes.

Northern Runes.

Northern Runes, from the " codex runicus."

German Runes.

EXAMPLES OF RUNIC ALPHABETS.

S

SAEHRIMNIR (Sooty) The magic boar that was killed, cooked by ANDHRIMNIR (Sooty Faced) in the giant cauldron ELDHRIMNIR (soot blackened) and eaten by the gods and heroes at VALHALLA. (See also BOAR.)

SAEMUND Medieval Icelandic bishop. At one time it was thought that he had written the ancient manuscripts now known as part of the *Elder* or POETIC EDDA, but which in old references are called *Saemund's Edda*.

SAEMUND'S EDDA See POETIC EDDA.

SAGA An Old Norse word meaning "story." The sagas were stories in prose or verse dating from the early 11th to the mid-14th centuries, first written down about 1200. They consisted of family sagas about early Icelandic settlers; sagas of the kings, which were semihistorical stories about the kings of Norway; and heroic sagas, which told of legendary heroes and fantastic adventures. The VOLSUNGA SAGA, (late 13th-century), is a good example of a heroic saga. Wagner's 19th-century operatic dramas in the RING OF THE NIBELUNG cycle were based on the adventures of hero SIGURD in the *Volsunga Saga*.

SAXO GRAMMATICUS Danish scholar of the 13th century who wrote GESTA DANORUM, a multivolume, partly mythical history of the Danes. In it Saxo recounts many myths of Denmark (including that of Hamlet) and Norway. Saxo's approach to the myths and the people in them was rather harsh and unsympathetic compared to that of Icelandic SNORRI STURLUSON. Nevertheless, *Gesta Danorum* is a valuable source for Norse myths.

SERPENT Word often used in mythology, religion and folklore to denote nonspecific reptiles, such as snakes and dragons and also sea monsters. In the Judeao-Christian tradition and in art, the serpent is a symbol of evil and of Satan or the Devil. In the Old Testament Bible (Genesis 3:1–6), the serpent is described as "more subtil than any beast of the field": It tempts Eve to eat fruit of the forbidden tree of knowledge. She shares the fruit with Adam, and the two are then banished from the Garden of Eden. The serpent, in verse 14, is cursed by God to creep about the earth on its belly and to eat dust for the rest of its life. Sometimes the serpent is seen as a symbol of regeneration, for it periodically sheds its skin and then appears to be reborn. In Irish lore Saint Patrick (whose anniversary is celebrated on March 17) is supposed to have rid Ireland of all snakes with his holy staff. In Norse mythology the DRAGON NITHOG chews at the roots of the sacred tree YGGDRASIL, and JORMUNGAND, the Midgard Serpent, encircles the earth with his tail in his mouth and spews poisonous fumes at RAGNAROK. The great god, ODIN, turns himself into a serpent to enter the cave where he will find "The Mead of Poetry" (see under ODIN); and FAFNIR turns himself into a dragon to guard his treasure (see "Otter's Ransom," under OTTER). A serpent is placed over LOKI's head after the gods have bound him to a rock. (See "Loki's Punishment," under LOKI.)

SESSRUMNIR (Many Seats) The hall of the goddess FREYA in Folkvang in ASGARD. In it she welcomed the slain heroes that she shared with the war god ODIN's VALHALLA.

SHINING MANE (Skinfaxi) The name of DAY's lead horse, whose gleaming mane lights up heaven and earth. (See "Night and Day," under CREATION.)

SHIPS AND SHIP BURIALS Ships were an important part of Norse culture. The Norsemen depended on ships not only for fishing and trading, but for expanding their empires. The

VIKING seafarers roamed from their northern strongholds as far south as the Iberian peninsula (modern Spain and Portugal), Italy and Sicily and the south of France, and as far east as Russia, Constantinople and Baghdad. It was a Viking navigator, Leif Ericsson, who "discovered" lands in North America in about the year 1000, almost five centuries before Christopher Columbus set foot in the Americas. The Vikings also colonized Iceland and Greenland.

Viking ships were longships, with graceful, upward-curving bows and sterns, often carved with elaborate designs. They were powered by oarsmen and sails.

Ships were so venerated that when a distinguished person died, he was put aboard his ship, which was then set afire and sent out to sea. In the myth of BALDER, Balder was set aboard his ship, RINGHORN, along with his dead wife, his horse, and some of his treasures. *Ringhorn* was then set afire and sent out to sea. In recent years archaeological digs have uncovered various burial ships in Scandinavia and England. Along with the bones of dead people and animals, they contained ancient weapons, chariots, jewelry, ornaments, food and utensils—all the necessities for the comfort of the dead in the after life. At Sutton Hoo, in East Anglia, England, the remains of an 80-foot ship were uncovered that had all the treasures but no bones of the dead. It is thought that the hero may have disappeared at sea, or perhaps he had been given a Christian burial while his treasures were buried according to a more ancient pagan custom. The Sutton Hoo ship dates from the 7th century. Other graves found in East Anglia were the tombs of humble people, even of children who were buried with toylike ships. In early English literature the account in *Beowulf* (written down about 1000 A.D.) describes the voyage of Skyld, first king of the Danes, on his funeral ship. In Egyptian mythology a ship was the vessel upon which a soul traveled from earth to heaven. Models of ships were placed in or beside the graves of the pharaohs.

The ship was so important in Norse culture that it was carried as a symbol in processions long after Christianity had become established. Medieval craftsmen built mock ships (symbols of life and of death and of the journey in between) to be carried in religious processions.

So beautiful and elaborate were these ships that eventually they were made collapsible; they could be folded up and stored inside the church until the next procession. It is thought that this medieval practice may have influenced the description of SKIDBLADNIR, the marvelous ship made for the god FREY. *Skinbladnir* could be shrunken down and folded to fit inside a pouch when not in use.

SIEGFRIED The hero of Germanic legend. See SIGURD.

SIF THOR's golden-haired wife, goddess of grain and of fertility. She was the mother of ULL, Thor's stepson. The mischiefmaker, LOKI, cut off Sif's hair while she slept. He was forced to replace it with strands of gold crafted by the DWARFS. (See THE TREASURES OF THE DWARFS.)

SIGURD (Siegfried in German) A human hero of Germanic legend, possibly of historical origin. He is the chief character in the 13th-century VOLSUNGA SAGA, in *Reginsmal*, (POETIC EDDA), in the German epic *The Nibelung*, and in the 19th-century opera drama THE RING OF THE NIBELUNG by Richard Wagner. The Sigurd stories are prefaced by the Norse myth "Otter's Ransom" (see under OTTER), though it is believed that originally there was no connection between the two.

SIGYN (SIGUNN, SIGRYN, SIGUNA) (Victory Giver) The wife of the trickster god, LOKI, and the mother of NARVI and VALI.

When the gods finally trapped Loki and bound him, placing a serpent over his head, Sigyn stayed by her husband's side. In a bowl she caught the venom that dripped from the serpent's jaws. But when she turned aside to empty the bowl, some venom fell on Loki and he writhed with pain, causing earthquakes on earth. Sigyn stayed with Loki until RAGNAROK, the end of the world. (See "Loki's Punishment," under LOKI.)

SIMUL The pole on which BIL AND YUKI carry their pail of water. (See "Sun and Moon," under CREATION.)

GOKSTADSKIBET

THIS GRACEFUL VESSEL, FOUND AT THE GOKSTAD, NORWAY, BURIAL SITE, PROBABLY BELONGED TO A 9TH-CENTURY VIKING CHIEFTAIN.

LOYAL SIGUNA, LOKI'S WIFE, CATCHES VENOM FROM THE
SERPENT THAT HANGS OVER LOKI'S HEAD.

IN THIS 12TH-CENTURY CARVING FROM HYLESTAD,
NORWAY, REGIN, THE SMITH, REPAIRS SIGURD'S
SWORD.

SINDRI A DWARF, the brother of BROKK. In
their underground realm, SVARTALFHEIM, the
dwarfs crafted numerous treasures for the gods.
(See THE TREASURES OF THE DWARFS.)

SINDRI (2) The name of one of the halls that
rose up after RAGNAROK.

SINGASTEIN The place where LOKI and
HEIMDALL, transformed into seals, fought over
the necklace Loki had stolen. (See "Freya and
the Golden Necklace," under FREYA.)

SKADE or SKADI (Destruction) Daughter of
the frost giant THIAZZI and wife of NIORD, the
VANIR god of the seas, of sailors and of fishermen. Skade was the goddess of winter, skiers
and hunters. After her father's death she went
to ASGARD, the home of the gods, to choose a
husband from among them. (See "Skade and
Niord," below.) She and Niord found that they
couldn't live happily together, for Skade didn't

like Niord's seashore home, NOATUN; and
Niord didn't like the bleak cold of THRYMHEIM,
Skade's home. It was Skade, in the story of
"Loki's Punishment" (see under LOKI), who
placed the venomous serpent over the head of
the trickster god. She is the personification of
the cold-hearted northern winter that can be
touched only briefly by the warmth of the summer sun (Niord) and the cheerful hearth fire
(Loki).

Skade and Niord In the PROSE EDDA the
story of the marriage between SKADE, goddess

of winter, and NIORD, the god associated with the seas and seafarers, follows immediately on "Idunn's Apples," (see under IDUNN), in which THIAZZI, Skade's father, is killed by the gods after stealing the apples. At the news of his death, Skade was full of rage. She put on her shining armor and her weapons and strode across BIFROST to ASGARD, the home of the AESIR.

The gods were at peace, glad to feel young again now that Idunn was back with her magic apples of youth. They asked Skade if she would take gold in payment for her father's death, for such was the custom of the Norsemen.

But Skade scornfully replied that she had all the gold she needed. When OLVALDI, Thiazzi's father, had died, he had left much gold to his sons Thiazzi, GANG, and IDI, and now she had all Thiazzi's share. Instead, she demanded a husband from among the gods.

Hastily the gods conferred and agreed it would be wise to let the icy giantess have her way. There was one condition. Skade must choose her husband by the look of his feet, not by his face.

Skade agreed. She, too, had a condition. The gods must make her laugh, for she was full of rage and her heart was cold.

The strange bargain was struck, and the gods stood barefoot behind a curtain that hid all but their feet. One pair of feet at once struck Skade as more beautiful than the rest. They must belong to the beautiful god, BALDER, she thought. She announced her choice.

Then out stepped NIORD, the VANIR god, lord of the seas and of seafarers, and the father of FREY and FREYA.

Skade was disappointed. Bitterly, she asked the gods to make her laugh.

LOKI, the trickster god who had been partially responsible for Thiazzi's death, had set his quick mind to work as soon as he had heard Skade's requests. Now he led forward one of THOR's rambunctious billygoats, and the two played such lively and hilarious antics that Skade and all the gods laughed until their sides ached.

As a wedding present for Skade, ODIN took Thiazzi's eyes from his pouch and hurled them into the heavens, where they shone brightly ever after as twin stars.

SKADE CHOSE HER HUSBAND BY POINTING TO THE FEET THAT SHE LIKED BEST.

Niord took his new wife to his home, NOA-TUN, by the seashore. But Skade didn't like the sunshine, the sea, the sound of the waves or the cry of the gulls.

Niord then went with Skade to THRYMHEIM, her sunless, freezing mountain home, but Niord didn't like the howling of the wolves, the wind, the bare mountains or the terrible cold.

The two tried to divide their time between the two homes: nine days in Niord's Noatun and nine in Skade's Thrymheim. But Skade spent more and more time in the cold mountains, a dark shape speeding over the snow in her snowshoes, bringing death to wolves and bears from her quiverful of arrows. She is the goddess of skiers and hunters.

The god of winter and of skiers and hunters is ULL, son of SIF and stepson of Thor, but, as far as we know, Skade and Ull never met.

Although Skade was made to laugh, for a moment, by the antics of Loki and the goat, she was the one who in the end placed the venomous serpent over Loki's head when he was bound to the rocks underground (see "Loki's Punishment," under LOKI.) She personifies the cold and heartlessness of the northern winter, which can be warmed only briefly by the summer sun (Niord) and the cheerful hearth fire (Loki in his more benign personification).

SKALDSKAPARMAL (Poetic Diction) A section in the PROSE EDDA; the source of "The Mead of Poetry" (see under ODIN).

SKIDBLADNIR (Wooden-Bladed) The magic ship made by the dwarfs, sons of IVALDI, and brought to FREY by LOKI. (See THE TREASURES OF THE DWARFS.) The ship was big enough to hold all the gods and their horses and equipment, and yet small enough to be folded up and put away in a pouch when not in use. It could sail over land or through the air, as well as on the sea, and has been compared to a swift-moving cloud or a magic carpet. (See SHIPS AND SHIP BURIALS.)

SKINFAXI (Shining Mane) The name of DAY's lead horse, whose gleaming mane lights up heaven and earth. (See "Night and Day," under CREATION.)

SKIRNIR (Shining) The servant of the shining god, FREY. He borrowed Frey's horse and sword and went on a long journey to woo the JOTUN maid, GERDA, for his lovesick master. (See "Frey and Gerda," under FREY.) In another myth Skirnir was sent by the gods to ask the DWARFS to make them a magic chain with which to bind the wolf, FENRIS.

"SKIRNIR'S JOURNEY" Poem in the *Codex Regius*, which forms part of the POETIC EDDA. The poem, in Icelandic called "For Skirnis," tells of SKIRNIR's wooing of GERDA for his master, FREY. (See "Frey and Gerda," under FREY.)

"SKIRNISMAL" ("The Lay of Skirnis") Poem in the *Arnamagnean Codex*, which forms part of the POETIC EDDA. Like "For Skirnis," (see

"SKIRNIR'S JOURNEY"), it tells the story of SKIRNIR's journey to woo the JOTUN maid, GERDA, for his master, FREY; in the *Arnamagnean Codex* the story is incomplete. (See "Frey and Gerda," under FREY.)

SKOLL The terrible wolf, born in IRONWOOD, who pursues the chariot of the sun and in the end, at RAGNAROK, devours it. (See "Sun and Moon," under CREATION.)

SKRYMIR (Big Fellow) A very large giant encountered by THOR and LOKI and their servants on their way to UTGARD. Skrymir, sometimes called VASTY in English retellings, was in fact UTGARD-LOKI in disguise. He was so huge that Thor and his companions mistook his mitten for a large cabin, where they spent the night. (See "Thor's Journey to Utgard," under THOR.)

SKULD (Future) One of the three NORNS, or Fates. She wears a veil and carries a scroll in her hands.

SKY In the Norse CREATION myth, the sky was made from the dome of the giant YMIR's skull. It was held up at the corners by four DWARFS, NORDI, SUDRI, AUSTRI and WESTRI. It was lighted by the sun and the moon, (see "Sun and Moon," under CREATION), and the stars created from sparks borrowed from MUSPELL-HEIM, the land of fire, and shaded by clouds made from Ymir's brains.

SKYBELLOWER (Heaven Bellower, also known as Himinbrioter or Himinhrjot) Black ox killed by THOR and used as bait to catch JORMUNGAND, the Midgard Serpent. (See "Thor and Hymir Go Fishing," under THOR.)

SLAVIN (Iron Cool) The fireproof shield placed by the gods between the sun and the two horses that pulled the chariot of the maiden SOL, who rode across the skies with the sun. (See "Sun and Moon," under CREATION.)

SLEIPNIR (Glider) ODIN's eight-legged horse, the offspring of SVADILFARI and LOKI, the shape-changer god who disguised himself as a mare to tempt Svaldifalri away from his work.

THE GIANT SKRYMIR (UTGARD-LOKI) TOWERS OVER THE GOD THOR.

(See "Asgard's Wall and the Giant Builder," under ASGARD.) Sleipnir was no ordinary horse. He could gallop over the sea and through the air as well as on land, and could outrun any horse in all the NINE WORLDS, including GOLD MANE (see "Thor's Duel with Hrungnir," under THOR). Sleipnir was able to journey to the world of the dead: He carried both HERMOD and ODIN there (see BALDER). At RAGNAROK, the end of the world, Sleipnir carried Odin into battle and was presumably killed by FENRIS, the wolf, along with his master. Eight-legged steeds occur in the folklore of many countries, including Siberia and India. Artists sometimes used a number of legs on an animal to suggest speed.

SNAKE An elongated, legless reptile of the order Squamata. (See SERPENT.)

SNORRI STURLUSON (1178–1241) A leading figure in Norse literature, Snorri was Iceland's most distinguished author. He was the author of the PROSE EDDA, of *Heimskringla* (a history of Norwegian kings), and of "Hattatal" (a poem in praise of King Haakon and Duke Skuli of Norway), plus various sagas. One of Iceland's greatest chieftains, Snorri came from the powerful Sturlung dynasty. He was educated at Iceland's foremost cultural center, Oddi, where he received strong training in law, history, poetry and the telling of sagas. He became renowned as a lawyer and a skald (poet). Politically ambitious, Snorri was welcomed at all the Scandinavian courts. He acquired great wealth and power, but was involved in numerous disputes and battles. He was finally slain in a political coup at the command of the king of Norway.

It would be difficult to exaggerate the importance of the *Prose Edda*, sometimes called the *Younger Edda* or the *Snorra Edda*. It gives us the only complete picture of Norse mythology dating from the Middle Ages. The *Prose Edda* had great influence on medieval Icelandic literature and helped to preserve the ancient scaldic tradition. Snorri's wit, tolerance and fine sense of style make the *Prose Edda* delightful reading.

SOEG The pail in which BIL AND YUKI carry water. (See "Sun and Moon," under CREATION.)

SOL Daughter of MUNDILFARI, sister of MANI, the man of the moon. Both were stolen away from MUNDILFARI by the gods, who put them to work in the heavens. Sol carries the sun in her chariot. Her horses are ARVAKR (EARLY WAKER) and ALSVID (All-Swift). Because the flaming heat of the sun would burn up any living thing that came too close, the gods placed an indestructible shield, SLAVIN (Iron Cool), between the horses and the sun.

The sun's chariot is forever pursued by a huge, evil wolf, SKOLL, who in the end (at RAGNAROK) will catch and devour the sun. (See "Sun and Moon," under CREATION.)

SOLSTICE The times of the year when the sun reaches its extreme northern and southern points in its journey across the heavens. The summer solstice is around June 21; the winter solstice is around December 22. The word *solstice* is made up of two Latin words, *sol*, meaning "sun," and *sistit*, meaning "stands." The sun appears to stand still before it turns back on its apparent course, and we have the longest day (summer solstice) and the shortest day (winter solstice) of the year. Both these days are times of rejoicing, especially in Norse countries. MIDSUMMER EVE, on June 21, was Balder's Day, celebrated with bonfires and the observance of sunrise and sunset. YULETIDE occurred at the time of the winter solstice, when people celebrated the beginning of the end of the winter months.

SON A jar. One of the three containers into which the DWARFS poured "The Mead of Poetry" (see under ODIN). The other containers were called BODN and ODRORIR.

SPIDER An arachnid (not an insect) that spins webs to trap food and to make its nests. The intricacy of the webs and the patience of the spider have fascinated people since ancient times. Spiders appear in many mythologies, including the African tale of Anansi and the Greek tale of Arachne. In Norse mythology spiders are associated with the NORNS, or Fates, who spin the webs of destiny for all living creatures.

STARS After they had created the earth and the sky, ODIN and his brothers caught glowing embers and sparks from MUSPELLHEIM and threw them up into the sky to be stars. As time went on, new stars were created. (See AURVANDIL; RAGNAROK; "The Sky," under CREATION; THIAZZI.)

STURLUSON See SNORRI STURLUSON.

SUDRI (South) One of the four DWARFS who held up the SKY (see CREATION).

SUN AND MOON See CREATION.

SURT (Black) The fire god with the flaming sword who will set fire to the world at RAGNAROK. He is called the leader of the sons of MUSPELLHEIM, land of fire. Surt and the god FREY fought a long battle at Ragnarok, and Surt killed Frey.

SURTSEY An island south of and belonging to Iceland, named for the Norse fire god, SURT. It was formed by a volcanic eruption from an underwater volcano, Sutur. The eruption began in 1963 and ended in 1967. Surtsey, the newest island on earth, is now a nature reserve where scientists study how life begins on a new island.

SUTTUNG (Heavy with Broth) A giant. He was the son of GILLING, who was murdered by the DWARFS FJALAR and GALAR. He was the brother of BAUGI. His daughter was GUNLOD, the guardian of "The Mead of Poetry" (see under ODIN). Suttung hid the three containers of the MEAD in an underground cave of the mountain HNITBORG where he and Gunlod lived. He would share it with no one. But ODIN, using his magic, succeeded in getting into the cave and stealing away the mead. Suttung was able to change himself into an eagle to chase Odin (who was also in eagle form), but he fell into a fire that the gods had made at the walls of ASGARD, their home, and perished.

SVADILFARI The stallion belonging to the giant HRIMTHURS who built the ASGARD wall. Svadilfari was a mighty animal, immensely powerful. He was lured from his task of helping the builder by a pretty mare (LOKI in disguise) and became the sire of SLEIPNIR, ODIN's eight-legged horse. (See "Asgard's Wall and the Giant Builder," under ASGARD.)

SVALIN (Iron Cool) The shield placed in SOL's chariot to protect her from the flames of the sun. (See "Sun and Moon," under CREATION.)

SVARTALFHEIM (also called Darkalfheim) The realm of the black, or dark, elves, who were also called DWARFS. It lay deep underground, beneath the roots of the World Tree, YGGDRASIL. It was here that LOKI came to ask the dwarfs, who were skilled craftsmen, to produce treasures for the gods. (See THE TREASURES OF THE DWARFS.)

SURTSEY IS THE NEWEST ISLAND ON EARTH. IT IS NAMED AFTER SURT, THE FIRE GIANT OF NORSE MYTH.

SVIPDAG (Swift Day) The human son of the seeress GROA and the hero of "The Ballad of Svipdag" ("SVIPDAGSMAL") in the POETIC EDDA. Svipdag goes to the underworld (NIFL-HEIM) to seek the advice of Groa. He summoned her up from the grave to ask her the best way to woo and win MENGLAD, the fair maiden he loves. Groa chants him a series of charms that will protect him in his travels. Svipdag sets off to seek Menglad. In JOTUNHEIM he finds a mas-sive gate guarded by the giant FJOLSVID. After a series of questions and answers, in which Svipdag learns about the gods and giants and their worlds, the giant finally lets Svipdag enter the gates, where he finds the beautiful Menglad waiting for him with open arms.

"SVIPDAGSMAL" ("The Ballad of Svipdag")
See SVIPDAG.

T

TANNGNIOST (Toothgnasher) One of the two fierce billy goats that drew the cart of the god THOR. The other goat was TANNGRISNER (Toothgrinder). The rumble of the cart was heard as thunder by people on earth. Thor's goats could be killed and eaten and then revived again the next day. (See "Thor's Journey to Utgard," under THOR.)

TANNGRISNIR (Toothgrinder) One of the two fierce billy goats that drew the cart of the god THOR. The other goat was TANNGNIOST (Toothgnasher). The rumble of the cart was heard as thunder by people on earth. Thor's goats could be killed and eaten and then revived again the next day. (See "Thor's Journey to Utgard," under THOR.)

THIALFI Son of the farmer Egil and brother of ROSKVA. He became THOR's servant because he disobeyed Thor's command not to break any of the bones of the goats on which he and his family were feasting in "Thor's Journey to Utgard," (see under THOR). Thialfi was long-legged and fleet of foot, but he was outrun in a race with HUGI (Thought) in Utgard. Thialfi was also Thor's companion in the duel with the giant HRUNGNIR; he easily vanquished the clay giant, MISTCALF, which the stone-headed giants had created in an attempt to frighten Thor. (See "Thor's Duel with Hungnir," under THOR.)

THIAZZI or TJASSE A powerful storm giant, son of OLVALDI, brother of GANG and IDI, father of SKADE. He lived in THRYMHEIM. Disguised as an eagle, Thiazzi tricked LOKI into helping him kidnap IDUNN, the goddess in charge of the magic apples of youth. In turn, Loki tricked the giant and brought Idunn back to ASGARD. Thiazzi was killed at the gates of Asgard (see "Idunn's Apples," under IDUNN). His daughter, Skade, was given the Vanir god, NIORD, as compensation for her father's death. The great god ODIN threw Thiazzi's eyes into the heavens to stay there forever as gleaming stars. (See "Skade and Niord," under SKADE.)

THOKK (Coal) The giantess who refused to weep for BALDER, thus ensuring that he would remain in HEL's realm until RAGNAROK. Some mythologists believe that Thokk was LOKI, the trickster god, in disguise. Thokk personifies the darkness of the underground (where coal is formed) that will not weep for the light of the sun (Balder).

THOR (Thunderer) The god of thunder and storms. His father was ODIN, his mother FJOR-GYN (Earth). Thor had two wives: JARNSAXA (Ironstone), who gave him two sons, MODI and MAGNI; and golden-haired SIF, who gave him two daughters, LORA or LORRIDE and THRUD. His realm was THRUDHEIM (or Thrudvang); his hall was BILSKIRNIR (lightning), which had 540 rooms, fittingly large for this giant of a god who loved to feast and entertain. Thor was strong and fiery of temper but he was well loved by the gods, respected by the giants and worshiped by the ordinary people.

Thor didn't ride a horse. Instead he had a chariot pulled by two enormous billy goats, TANNG-NIOST and TANNGRISNIR. The wheels of the chariot made a noise like thunder when Thor roared across the heavens.

Thor's greatest possession was his hammer, MJOLLNIR. When he hurled it, the hammer would always hit its mark and then return to Thor like a boomerang. Mjollnir was not only a weapon but a symbol of fertility, used at weddings, and of resurrection, used at burials. Thor also had iron gauntlets with which he could crush rocks, and a belt, MEGINGJARDIR, which doubled his mighty strength.

At RAGNAROK, the end of the world, Thor kills JORMUNGAND, the Midgard Serpent, his ancient enemy, but himself is killed by the poisonous fumes of the dying serpent.

Worship of Thor continued for centuries after

THOR IS SHOWN HERE WITH HIS MAGIC HAMMER, MJOLLNIR.

THOR RODE A CHARIOT PULLED BY TWO BILLY GOATS. THE WHEELS OF THE CART MADE A NOISE LIKE THUNDER AND LIGHTNING FLASHED AROUND THEM.

the coming of Christianity. The great OAK trees of central and western Europe were sacred to the god. Worshipers of Thor made wooden oak chairs with high backs ("high seats") to ensure Thor's blessing on the house (protecting it from lightning) and the well-being and fruitfulness of the family and its lands. As well as bringing thunder and lightning and storms, Thor sent the rain that made the fields fertile.

Evidence of Thor's popularity is found in the name THURSDAY (the fifth day of the week), and in numerous place names, such as Thundersley, in Essex, Thunderfield, Surrey, Thundridge, Hertfordshire, and many others in England and elsewhere.

There are many myths about Thor (see below) taken from the POETIC EDDA and the PROSE EDDA; in Richard Wagner's RING OF THE NIBELUNG Thor appears as Donner; Thor is also found in Henry Wadsworth Longfellow's "Saga of King Olaf," part of *Tales of a Wayside Inn*.

The Theft of Thor's Hammer Thor is the god of thunder and the personification of strength and manliness. His hammer, MJOLL-

NIR, is a potent weapon, the gods' only real defense against the giants. Thor is seldom separated from his hammer, so it is not surprising that he went into a fury when the hammer disappeared.

LOKI, the trickster god, heard Thor's shouts and knew that for once he must help rather than be mischievous. He rushed to FREYA, the beautiful goddess, and borrowed her suit of falcon feathers. Then Loki flew to JOTUNHEIM, the home of the giants.

THRYM, the huge and ugly king of the frost giants, was in a good mood, plaiting gold thread to make leashes for his colossal hounds. He greeted Loki cheerfully. Loki asked him if he had stolen Thor's hammer, and the giant admitted that he had. With a chilling laugh he said that he had hidden it eight miles under the earth where no one would find it. The only way to get it back would be to send him Freya as his bride.

Even Loki was shocked at the thought of sending the fair goddess to this monster. He flew quickly back to ASGARD on his falcon wings and told Thor the news. Then together they went to Freya and told her of the giant's request.

Freya was so furious and agitated that she broke the clasp of her golden BRISINGS' NECKLACE. The starry beads were scattered all over the floor. Never, never would she be the bride of Thrym, she vowed.

Then all the gods got together for a meeting. They knew that it was only a matter of time until all the giants found out that Thor no longer had his hammer and would come marching on ASGARD. The gods were worried.

Only HEIMDALL, the watchman who stood at BIFROST, the rainbow bridge, and could see far into the future, remained calm.

He said that Thor must be dressed as a bride and go to meet Thrym.

The gods roared with laughter at the thought of the mighty, red-bearded Thor dressed as a woman, and Thor let out a shout of rage. But gradually he saw the wisdom of the plan and allowed the goddesses to fit his large frame into a long dress and drape a veil over his shaggy head. Freya's necklace was repaired and placed around his thick neck, a girdle hung with jingling keys encircled his waist and his manly chest was covered with glittering jewels.

Loki was dressed as a bridesmaid. Together the peculiar pair climbed into Thor's chariot and the two billy goats took off at great speed, making the wheels rumble like thunder.

Thrym was overjoyed when he heard that Freya was on her way. He ordered the halls to be swept, new straw laid down and a gargantuan feast to be prepared. He said to himself, "I have cattle with golden horns, and jet-black oxen, and now I'll have Freya. What more could any giant want?"

Thor was well known for his great appetite, but Thrym was astonished to see what he thought was a maiden eating such huge helpings of fish and meat and downing large goblets of mead. Quick-witted Loki explained that the bride had not eaten or drunk for eight days, so anxious was she to meet her groom.

Delighted, Thrym reached over to lift the bride's veil and kiss her. But when he saw Thor's flashing, red-rimmed eyes glaring at him through the veil, he fell back in dismay.

Once again sly Loki whispered an explana-tion. The bride had not had a wink of sleep for eight nights, so anxious was she for her wedding night.

At that, Thrym ordered that the hammer be brought to his bride and the wedding ceremony commence at once. (It was the custom of the Norsemen to invoke the blessing of Thor's hammer at their weddings.)

No sooner was Mjollnir placed upon his lap than Thor leapt up, tore off his veil and started to slay every giant in sight.

And that was how Thor got back his hammer and made Asgard safe from the giants once again.

The only source of this myth is the poem "THRYMSKVITHA" ("The Lay of Thrym") from the POETIC EDDA. It is considered a masterpiece of burlesque.

Thor and the Giant Geirrod The tale of how the god Thor destroyed the formidable giant GEIRROD and his two fearsome daughters is a popular myth, told in many versions. In this one, LOKI, ever the trickster, persuades Thor to accompany him to the giant's castle.

One day Loki put on a suit of falcon feathers and flew to the hall of the giant Geirrod, one of the meanest of the JOTUNS. Geirrod caught sight of the handsome falcon and ordered the bird to be brought to him.

It took several of the TROLLS to capture Loki, for he hopped about the wall, always just out of reach. But when at last he tried to take flight, he found himself stuck fast to the wall by some evil spell.

He was set before Geirrod, who knew at once that this was not a real falcon. He locked Loki in a cage and kept him without food and water until at last Loki confessed who he was. The giant set Loki free on the condition that he would bring him the thunder god, Thor, without any of his weapons. Faint with hunger, Loki agreed to bring Thor to Geirrod. Off he flew, his trickster's mind already devising a plan.

Once safe in ASGARD, Loki prattled on to anyone who would listen about the wonders of Geirrod's castle, and how the giant was eager to meet the mighty Thor, to introduce him to his two beautiful daughters, GIALP and GREIP and to entertain him royally. Of course, Thor heard the gossip, and being a simple soul, he couldn't long resist the temptation to visit Geirrod, his new admirer.

At Loki's urging, he left his weapons, even the magic hammer, MJOLLNIR, behind and set forth, with Loki at his side to show the way. As the distance was long, they stayed overnight with the kindly giantess GRID. She was friendly to the AESIR gods and liked Thor. When Loki had gone to sleep, she warned Thor about Geirrod and loaned him her belt of power and her magic staff.

The next day when Thor and Loki were crossing the rushing torrent of the VIMUR, the river began to rise higher and higher. Thor hung onto the magic staff, and Loki hung onto Thor, almost drowning in the blood-red river. Up ahead Thor saw the giantess Gialp. It was she who was making the waters rise. Thor threw a rock at her, and she ran off, howling. Then Thor pulled himself to shore with the help of a small tree called the ROWAN, or mountain ash.

When they arrived at Geirrod's hall, Thor was shown into a small room. He sat down wearily in the only chair and closed his eyes. Suddenly he felt himself rising toward the roof. Quickly he rammed Grid's staff against the roof beam and pushed. Then down he came, right on top of Gialp and Greip, who had been trying to raise the chair and crush Thor against the roof. The two ugly, evil creatures were themselves crushed to death by Thor's weight.

Thor went straight to Geirrod's hall.

Geirrod shouted an ironic welcome, raising his hand in mock greeting and throwing a red-hot lump of iron at Thor.

Thor caught it in Grid's iron gloves and threw it back at Geirrod, who had leapt behind a pillar. The hot ball went right through the pillar, through Geirrod's head and through the wall into the yard, where it bored deep into the earth.

Thus Thor once more triumphed over treachery and guile—with the help of the giantess Grid, who was on the side of the gods.

This tale is told several times in Norse literature, including in the SKALDSKAPARMAL in the PROSE EDDA and in SNORRI STURLUSON's retelling of "THORSDRAPA."

Thor's Journey to Utgard This story is one of the best known of the Norse myths, rich in comedy and suspense and with an undercurrent of magic and terror.

One day the god THOR decided to go to UTGARD, stronghold of the largest giants in JOTUNHEIM. Because its chief, UTGARD-LOKI, was known to be a master of trickery, Thor brought along ASGARD's own trickster god, LOKI, as a companion.

As it grew dark Thor's chariot, drawn by two lively billy goats, stopped at a small farmhouse. The farmer and his wife were very poor and had little to eat. With a wave of his magic hammer, MJOLLNIR, Thor killed TANNGNIOST and TANNGRISNIR, his goats, and put them on the fire to cook.

Thor told the peasants to eat their fill when the meat was ready, but to be sure not to break any of the bones. They should be placed carefully onto the goatskins that Thor had stretched on the floor.

THIALFI, the farmer's son, disobeyed Thor (perhaps at the mischievous urging of Loki) and cracked a leg bone to suck out the delicious marrow.

Next morning, when Thor was ready to leave, he waved Mjollnir over the piles of bone and skin and up sprang the goats, as lively as ever. But one of them had a limp. Thor yelled in fury, for he knew that someone had disobeyed him. However, he accepted the terrified farmer's offer and took Thialfi and his sister, ROSKVA, to be his servants. He left the goats with the farmer to be taken care of until his return and set off on foot.

Thor and Loki and the two youngsters journeyed all day. That night they came to a forest in Jotunheim where the trees were so tall that their tops were lost in the clouds. They saw a strangely shaped cabin that seemed to have no door. They crept inside to shelter from the cold and were soon asleep.

In the middle of the night they sprang awake as the earth shook, and there was a frightful crashing sound, followed by a steady rumble and a whistling wind. Even Thor was frightened. He, Loki and the youngsters crept into a narrow side room in the cavernous hall, Thor clutching his hammer to his chest.

At first light, Thor went outside and saw the cause of all the noise. At the foot of a tree lay the biggest giant Thor had ever seen. He was fast asleep and snoring mightily.

Thor put on the magic belt given to him by the giantess GRID to double his strength. He held his hammer even more firmly, though the giant was so big that Thor decided not to throw it hastily.

Soon the giant woke up. He picked up what the travelers had mistaken for a large cabin or cave. It was a giant glove. The side room was the thumb of the monster's mitten.

When the giant stood up, Thor and his companions had to crane their heads back to look at him. The giant introduced himself as SKRYMIR, sometimes called Big Fellow, or VASTY.

After they had eaten breakfast—a poor one for Thor and his friends, a huge one for Skrymir—they set off again, this time with the giant crashing through the trees ahead to show them the way to Utgard.

By nightfall they were exhausted and hungry. The giant flung down his huge food bag, telling the other travelers to help themselves.

But try as they might, Thor, Loki and the farmer's son and daughter couldn't untie the knots that secured the bag, so they lay down, hungry, and tried to shut out the sound of Skrymir's thunderous snores.

At last Thor couldn't stand it any longer. He hit Skrymir on the head with his hammer. Skrymir opened one eye and complained that a leaf had fallen on his head. He was asleep again in a second.

Furious, Thor hit him again.

Now Skrymir mumbled something about an acorn.

Beside himself, Thor took a running jump and hurled the hammer with all his might onto the giant's head.

Skrymir finally sat up and rubbed his head. He decided that there must be some birds above his head. Skrymir got up and picked up his bag. He told the travelers to watch their step in Utgard, for the giants there were *really* big.

The four travelers breathed a sigh of relief as Skrymir lumbered off through the trees.

When they reached Utgard, the giants had assembled to meet them. They decided to engage in contests with the travelers.

Loki immediately announced that no one could beat him at eating.

One of the giants placed a huge platter in front of Loki and sat down on the other side of it. The two began gobbling and in no time bumped heads as they met in the middle of the platter—or what was left of it. The giant had eaten his half of the wooden dish, along with all the bones, so he won the contest.

Next young Thialfi claimed that he was the fastest runner in the world.

Utgard-Loki called forth a young giant named HUGI. A racecourse was marked out.

Thialfi was indeed as swift as the wind, but he was no match for Hugi. Thialfi lost the race and retired to Loki's side, humiliated.

Something must be done to save face. Thor strode forward, claiming that he was well known as a mighty drinker.

The giants placed before him a long, curved horn. Confidently Thor took a huge draft. But when he looked at the horn, it was still brimming over with liquid. Once again he raised the horn to his lips. He opened his throat and let the liquid pour down until he was red in the face. But the horn was still almost full. After the third try Thor put down the horn, mortified and angry.

Utgard-Loki shook his head sadly, remarking that the mighty Thor wasn't so mighty, after all. Every one of his men could empty the horn at one draft. He suggested that Thor try his hand at something easier, like lifting a cat from the floor.

Grimly Thor put his hand under the cat's belly to lift it. But it felt as heavy as a ton of lead. By using both his hands and all the strength of his mighty arms, he was able to raise the cat so that one paw was an inch off the floor. Then he fell back, exhausted.

Angry at the laughter of the giants, Thor shouted that he was the finest wrestler in all Asgard and would take on anyone.

The giant shook his head doubtfully. He couldn't think of a JOTUN who would be bothered to fight such a weakling. Then he remembered his old foster mother, ELLI, and he summoned her to the hall.

Embarrassed, Thor put his hand out to grasp the arm of the skinny old crone, not meaning to hurt her. Suddenly he was flying through the air. He landed flat on his back. The wizened old woman cackled merrily and the giants shouted with laughter. Now Thor wrestled the old woman in earnest, but no matter what he did, the hag outplayed him, until at last he gave up and slunk away.

The next morning Utgard-Loki led the crestfallen travelers to the gates of Utgard. There, the giant admitted that he had practiced magic on them. First, he had disguised himself as Skrymir. He had used troll magic to tie the food bag with strands of iron. Then, when Thor thought he was hitting the giant's head with his hammer, he had been in fact hitting a hard rock. He told Thor that on his way home he would see the rock, a hillside with three very deep dents in it.

The giant said that in the contests, too, he had used spells and trickery:

LOGI, the giant who beat Loki in gluttony, was in fact Fire, which consumes everything in its path.

The runner, Hugi, was Thought—and no one can move as fast as thought.

The drinking horn was anchored in the seas of the world. No one can drain the oceans, but from then on, said the giant, the tides would ebb and flow, just as they had when Thor drank so mightily.

The cat was JORMUNGAND, the Midgard Serpent, who is so big that he encircles the world. When Thor had made the "cat" lift its paw, the serpent's back had almost touched the sky.

Thor was so angry at the trickery that he raised his hammer to strike the giant, but Utgard-Loki vanished into the air. So did the castle and its walls and all the other giants. It was as if they had never been.

Although in this myth Thor is upstaged by Utgard-Loki, he isn't totally humiliated, for he did create dents in the hillside and the ebbing and flowing of the tides. One senses that Thor was a favorite god among the Scandinavians. This is one of the longest and most richly told myths written by SNORRI STURLUSON in the PROSE EDDA, its only source.

Thor and Hymir Go Fishing The myth of the fishing expedition of the thunder god, THOR, and the giant HYMIR, and Thor's battle with JORMUNGAND, the Midgard Serpent, was a favorite and was retold many times, not only in Scandinavia. In Gosforth, England, carvings on two stone slabs clearly show Thor fishing with an ox's head and fighting with the serpent. The story begins (in this version) with the gods making merry, as they so often did.

There was nothing the AESIR gods liked better than to eat or drink. No sooner was one feast over than they were making plans for the next one. One evening they cast RUNES that told them that their next gathering should be at the abode of AEGIR, the JOTUN lord of the sea. Aegir lived under the waves with his wife, RAN.

Aegir complained that he didn't have a cauldron big enough to brew ale for all the gods. TYR, the one-handed god, declared that he knew where he could find a cauldron a mile deep. With Thor as his companion, Tyr set off to find Hymir, who lived east of ELIVAGAR in JOTUNHEIM, the land of giants.

When they came to Hymir's dwelling, their way was barred by an ogress with nine-hundred heads. But there was another jotun, beautiful and kind, and she welcomed Tyr as her son, and she welcomed Thor.

She said she would try to help them and advised them to hide underneath the biggest cauldron in the hall.

Hymir lumbered into the hall, icicles dangling from his bushy beard and his eyes sparkling dangerously. He sensed the presence of strangers.

The jotun woman explained that Tyr had come to visit and had brought a friend, and that they were hiding under the big cauldron, being a little nervous of Hymir.

Hymir's eyes swept the hall. At his ferocious glance pillars fell down and cauldrons shattered. But the biggest cauldron stayed whole, and Thor and Tyr crawled out unharmed.

Thor was an awesome sight, with his bristling red hair and beard. Hymir quickly ordered

IN THIS ANCIENT PICTURE, THOR GRAPPLES WITH THE MIDGARD SERPENT WHILE THE GIANT HYMIR CRINGES WITH TERROR.

three oxen to be killed for their supper. Thor, who was famous for his huge appetite, ate two of the oxen.

Hymir said that they would have to go hunting for the next meal. Thor suggested that they should fish for it instead.

For bait, Thor took the head of a mighty black ox, SKYBELLOWER. While Hymir rowed and caught a whale or two, Thor readied his tackle and cast his line into the water. Almost at once the terrible head of Jormungand, the Midgard Serpent, appeared above the waves, the ox's head in its mouth. Hymir's eyes bulged out in terror, but Thor coolly held the line and flung his hammer, MJOLLNIR, at the ghastly head. Again and again the hammer struck its mark and flew back to its master. Terrified, Hymir cut the line and the bloodied serpent sank beneath the waves.

Shaken, Hymir rowed back to the shore as fast as he could. Once safely on land, he decided to test Thor's strength. He asked him to either haul in the boat and tackle or carry the two whales up the cliff to the house.

Without wasting a word, Thor took hold of the boat, dragged it out of the water and carried it, whales and all, to the house.

Tyr and the jotun woman congratulated Thor on his feat of strength. But Hymir had yet another test for Thor. He handed him his goblet and asked him to try to break it.

Thor hurled the goblet at the wall. Stone and rubble tumbled from the hole made in the wall, but the goblet remained intact.

Thor threw the goblet over and over again until the hall was in ruins. Then the giant's lovely wife whispered to him to throw the goblet at Hymir's head, which was the hardest object for miles around.

And sure enough, when the goblet hit Hymir's stony head, it shattered into pieces, though the giant's head remained without a dent.

Then Hymir said that Thor could have the cauldron if he could carry it. Tyr tried to lift the cauldron but couldn't move it. But mighty Thor picked up the huge cauldron easily and wore it like a helmet. Then he and Tyr set off for home. On the way they were attacked by Hymir and many-headed jotuns, but Thor wielded his

magic hammer and put an end to Hymir and his ugly followers.

And so it was that the AESIR gods drank deep from Hymir's cauldron in AEGIR's halls for many a night to come. (See "Loki's Mocking," under LOKI, for one of those occasions.)

"The Lay of Hymir" is in *Hymiskvitha*, a poem of the POETIC EDDA, and part of SNORRI STURLUSON's PROSE EDDA.

Thor's Duel with Hrungnir   The story of the god THOR's duel with the mighty giant HRUNGNIR begins with a horse race between ODIN and the giant. On one of his journeys Odin, mounted on his eight-legged horse, SLEIPNIR, met HRUNGNIR, the strongest of the giants. Hrungnir challenged Odin to a race on his splendid horse, GULLFAXI (GOLDEN MANE).

Odin agreed and was off in a flash, with Hrungnir close behind.

Sleipnir knew the way home well and streaked through VALGRIND, the gate of VALHALLA, Odin's hall.

Gullfaxi was going too fast to be stopped until he and his master were well within ASGARD, the realm of the gods. The laws of hospitality dictated that the gods could not hurt their guest.

The goddess FREYA gave Hrungnir THOR's great drinking horn and filled it to the brim. (Thor, the thunder god, was away that day, fighting trolls in IRONWOOD.) Freya had to keep refilling the horn, for Hrungnir emptied it in huge gulps and soon became noisy and quarrelsome. He boasted that he would take all of VALHALLA under his arm and carry it back to JOTUNHEIM for a plaything. And he would take Freya and golden-haired SIF, Thor's wife, to be his own wives and servants.

At this the gods grew angry, and Odin had a hard time keeping them from attacking their unpleasant guest.

Just then Thor burst into the hall, brandishing MJOLLNIR, his hammer. He, too, wanted to attack the giant. Instead, he agreed to meet the giant at GIOTUNAGARD, the Place of Stones, to fight a duel.

Hrungnir clambered onto Gullfaxi and rode back to Jotunheim with the news. The giants were uneasy, even though Hrungnir was the strongest of them all. They put their thick heads together and came up with a plan. They would frighten Thor by making a huge clay giant, nine leagues high, out of clay. They named the clay giant Mokkuralfi, or MISTCALF, and put inside it the heart of a mare, which was the biggest heart they could find.

Hrungnir's heart was made of stone, sharp-edged and three-cornered. His head, too, was made of stone, and so were his shield and club. Together, Mistcalf and Hrungnir made a fearful sight as Thor and his servant, THIALFI, drew near.

Thialfi was quick-witted as well as fleet of foot. He ran up to the giant and advised him to hold his shield low rather than high, in case Thor attacked him from below. The stone-headed giant flung his shield to the ground and stood on it with his big feet. Then he threw his club at Thor.

Thor threw his thunderbolt hammer at the giant's head at the same time. Club and hammer met in midair with an awesome crack and a sizzling bolt of lightning.

The giant's stone club was shattered into a thousand pieces and fell to the earth, where to this day (it is said) the splinters may be found in quarries. They are mined by men to make WHETSTONES to hone, or sharpen, their edged tools. But Thor's hammer zoomed on and struck the giant, who immediately fell dead. His outflung leg pinned Thor's head to the ground.

Thialfi, who had already hacked Mistcalf to pieces, tried to release Thor, but the giant's leg was so huge and heavy that even when Odin and the other gods came to help, they couldn't move it an inch. Thor lay groaning, for a piece of whetstone had stuck in his head.

Now along came MAGNI, Thor's son who was only three years old but already enormous. He lifted Hrungnir's leg easily, and Thor was at last able to roll free. Thor gave Magni Hrungnir's horse, Gullfaxi, as a reward.

Thor's head still hurt, so he sent for the clever witch, GROA. She cast some RUNE stones, and whispered some magic words, and the pain went away. Thor was so relieved that he wanted to make Groa happy. He told her that he had rescued her lost husband, AURVANDIL. He had carried him across the poisonous stream, ELIVA-GAR. Now Aurvandil was safe and waiting for Groa.

Groa was so happy at the news that she ran from the hall. She couldn't spare the time to recall the magic spell that would remove the stone from Thor's head. To this day, it is said, no one is allowed to throw or drop a whetstone anywhere in the world, for it makes Thor's head ache all over again.

Hrungnir was the strongest of Thor's adversaries. Even so, the giants were uneasy about the outcome of the battle. With the defeat of Hrungnir, the war between the gods and the giants came to a turning point: Some mythologists believe that the giants now gave up hope of killing Thor and of storming Asgard.

This story is from SNORRI STURLUSON, PROSE EDDA; Snorri based his telling of this legend partly on the poem *Haustlong*.

"THORSDRAPA" A late 10th-century poem by poet Eilif Guthrunarson. SNORRI STURLU-SON included "Thorsdrapa" in his PROSE EDDA for an alternative version of the myth "Thor and the Giant Geirrod" (see under THOR).

THOUGHT Personified by the young giant HUGI, who outran fleet-footed THIALFI, THOR's servant, in the story "Thor's Journey to Utgard" (see under THOR).

In another guise, Thought was embodied as the raven, HUGIN, one of ODIN's faithful companions.

THRUD Daughter of the god THOR and his wife SIF. She was promised by the gods to the DWARF ALVIS. Her sister was LORA or LOR-RIDA.

THRUDHEIM (Place of Might) THOR's realm in ASGARD, sometimes called Thrudvang. It was the site of his huge hall, BILSKIRNIR.

THRUDVANG See THRUDHEIM.

THRYM A frost giant, sometimes called the king of the frost giants. He stole Thor's hammer and demanded the goddess FREYA for his wife if the hammer were to be returned. With the help of the trickster, LOKI, the hammer is won back at a wedding ceremony in which Thor is the "bride," and Thrym is killed by Thor. (See "The Theft of Thor's Hammer," under THOR.)

THRYMHEIM (Noisy Place) The mountain home of the giant THIAZZI and of his daughter, SKADE. It was a cold and lonely place, noisy with the howling of winds and of wolves. In the story of "Skade and Niord" (under SKADE), the god NIORD hated the place. The god LOKI came here to rescue IDUNN after she had been kidnaped by the giant THIAZZI.

"THRYMSKVITHA" ("The Lay of Thrym") A poem in the POETIC EDDA that is the only source of the story "The Theft of Thor's Hammer," (see under THOR).

THUND (Roaring) The torrent that runs outside VALHALLA.

THUNDER, GOD OF See THOR.

THURSDAY The fifth day of the week, named after the god THOR. The Romans named this day after their god Jove, who like Thor was associated with thunder. In French it is called *jeudi*, in Spanish *jueves*, in Italian *giovedi*.

TOOTHGNASHER See TANNGNIOST.

TOOTHGRINDER See TANNGRISNIR.

The TREASURES OF THE DWARFS The story of how the gods came to acquire the treasures for which they were famed is one of the most popular of the Norse myths. It starts when the mischievous LOKI creeps into the bedroom of SIF, THOR's wife, and cuts off her golden hair while she sleeps.

When the fierce god Thor discovered that Loki had cut off and stolen Sif's dazzling hair, Thor threatened to tear Loki into small pieces. But the sly trickster put on a fine show of remorse and promised to bring back not only hair made of real gold for Sif, but other treasures as well, so Thor let him go.

Loki immediately made his way to SVARTALFHEIM, the underworld caverns where the DWARFS lived. These misshapen, undersized creatures were ugly and bad-tempered, but they were master craftsmen when it came to mining and shaping gold and the other metals found in their darkling realm.

Loki went first to the cave of the sons of IVALDI. He begged them to make golden strands so real that they would grow out of Sif's head. This feat the dwarfs accomplished with their magic, and while the furnace was still hot they made other magical treasures for Loki to carry to the gods:

SKIDBLADNIR was a marvelous ship for FREYR. It could fold up small enough to fit into a pouch and yet expand to a size large enough to carry all the AESIR gods and their equipment. It could sail on land or sea or air.

For ODIN they made GUNGNIR, a strong and slender spear that always flew straight to its target.

On his way back Loki stopped at the cave of BROKK and SINDRI. These two dwarfs wanted to show that their work was much finer than that of the sons of Ivaldi. Loki was happy to let them try. The more treasures he brought back to the gods, the more they would feel like forgiving Loki for all his mischief. Loki bet his head that Brokk and Sindri couldn't do better work than the Ivaldi brothers.

Then, in spite of Loki's teasing (he turned himself into a gadfly and kept stinging poor Brokk as he pumped the bellows), the dwarfs made GULLINBRUSTI, a boar with bristles and mane of shining gold, which Loki gave to Frey, and DRAUPNIR, an arm ring of gold that, on every ninth night, dropped eight more rings just as beautiful as the first. Draupnir became Odin's favorite arm ring.

Finally the dwarfs produced MJOLLNIR, a massive iron hammer. The hammer had a short handle because the gadfly had made Brokk pause for an instant at the bellows. In spite of that, the hammer had the magic property of always reaching its mark and then returning at once to its owner, who would be Thor. A powerful weapon, indeed.

When Loki presented the treasures, the gods agreed that the wondrous hammer was the most powerful treasure of all, for it could guard the gods against the giants.

Brokk claimed that he was the winner of the bet and that Loki owed him his head. But as usual, Loki used fast talk and cunning and escaped with nothing worse than sore lips when Brokk tried to sew up his wicked mouth.

And Sif was delighted with her new growth of precious gold hair. Ever afterward the term "Sif's hair" was used in Norse myths as a kenning, or condensed metaphor, for "gold."

This story plays an important part in the Norse myths, for it makes clear the associations, such as Thor and his hammer and Odin and his spear, that had existed for as long as the gods had been known in Scandinavia. See the individual entries for the significance of each of the treasures.

TUESDAY The third day of the week. It is named after the one-handed war god, TYR. The Romans identified Tyr with their own god of war, Mars; they called the third day *dies Marti* (Mars' Day); it became *mardi* in French, *martes* in Spanish, and *martedi* in Italian.

TWILIGHT OF THE GODS See RAGNAROK.

TYR A god of war, a sky god, the bravest of the gods. He was concerned with justice and with fair treaties. It is thought that at one time Tyr was even more important then ODIN, and more ancient. But by the time the Norse myths were written down, Tyr's importance had diminished, and not much is known about him now. For example, in some stories (see "Thor and Hymir Go Fishing," under THOR) Tyr is the son of the giant HYMIR; in others he is the son of Odin.

Tyr was the only god brave enough and fairminded enough to put his hand into the jaws of the terrible wolf, FENRIS. (See "Fenris and the Gods," under FENRIS.) When the other gods broke their word to Fenris and tied him up, Fen-

ris bit off Tyr's hand. That is why Tyr is always depicted as the one-handed god.

At RAGNAROK, the end of the world, Tyr and GARM, the Hel Hound, kill one another.

Tuesday (in Old English *Tiwesdaeg*) was named after Tyr, who is also known as Tiw, Tiv, Ziv, or Tiwaz. His name means "shining one" and is synonymous with "god."

OF ALL THE GODS, TYR WAS THE ONLY ONE BRAVE ENOUGH TO FEED FENRIS, THE MONSTER WOLF.

U

ULL (or ULLER) The winter god of skiers and snowshoes, hunting, the bow and the shield. Son of the goddess SIF, stepson of THOR. YDALIR (Yew Dales) was his home. Not much is known about Ull, but he must have been important at one time for his name crops up in Scandinavian names of people and places.

URD (or WYRD) One of the three NORNS, or Fates, who spun on their web the destiny of all living beings. Urd, meaning "Past," was the most powerful of the three. The sacred WELL OF URD (or Wyrd) was named after her. She is the oldest of the three sisters and is usually pictured as looking backward to the past.

URD, WELL OF The well, also called "Wyrd," named after URD, the most powerful of the three NORNS. The sacred waters of the well help to protect Yggdrasil against the forces of evil.

The gods rode over BIFROST to hold all their important meetings at the Well of Urd.

One legend says that two swans lived in this magical well and that from them are descended all the swans in the world.

UTGARD (Outer Place) The capital of JOTUN-HEIM, the land of the giants. The stronghold was ruled by the giant king SKRYMIR, or UTGARD-LOKI. The god THOR was humiliated and defeated in Utgard by the magic of the giant king. (See "Thor's Journey to Utgard," under THOR.)

UTGARD-LOKI (Loki of the Outer World) The strongest and most cunning of the giants, also known as SKRYMIR. He humiliated and outwitted the gods THOR and LOKI and their servant THIALFI in the story "Thor's Journey to Utgard" (see under THOR). In some medieval Christian tales, Utgard-Loki personifies the devil.

V

"VAFTHRUDNIR" ("Vafthrudnismal") "The Lay of Vafthrudnir." A 10th-century Norse poem from the POETIC EDDA. Vafthrudnir is described as a "wise giant and riddle master." ODIN, using the name Gagnrad, goes to visit the giant to test his knowledge and to obtain some wisdom. The poem takes the form of a question-and-answer game between Odin and the giant. (This format was common in the Eddic poems.) First Odin (as Gagnrad) answers Vafthrudnir's questions; the giant is impressed by his guest's knowledge and in turn answers Odin's questions about the sun and the moon, day and night, winter and summer, the first giants, the VANIR gods, the hall of dead heroes, and the fate of the gods. Finally Odin asks him about the end of the world and the world thereafter. Odin in turn is impressed by the giant's knowledge and asks him how he acquired it. Vafthrudnir says that he has roamed far and wide, even to the home of the dead in NIFLHEIM, and can also read the RUNES.

"The Lay of Vafthrudnir" is a valuable source of information about the Norse myths. All of it appears in the CODEX REGIUS and some of it in the ARNAMAGNEAN CODEX. SNORRI STURLUSON draws upon it extensively in the PROSE EDDA.

"VAFTHRUDNISMAL" See "VAFTHRUDNIR."

VALA Seeress. (See VOLVA.)

VALASKIALF The great god ODIN's silver-roofed hall in ASGARD, the home of the gods. It was the site of HLIDSKIALF, the high seat from which Odin could observe all NINE WORLDS.

VALGRIND (Death's Gate) The outer gate of VALHALLA, the hall of the slain.

VALHALLA (Hall of the Slain) The hall built by the god ODIN in ASGARD to receive heroes slain in battle. The warriors, called EINHERIAR, fought all day and feasted all night. They were brought to Valhalla by the VALKYRIES, Odin's warrior maidens, led by the goddess FREYA. The heroes would go to battle at Odin's side at RAGNAROK, the end of the world, where all would be slain once again.

In modern English the word *Valhalla* means "a heavenly place where the deserving dead find eternal happiness, or an esteemed burial place on earth," such as Westminster Abbey in London, England, where many honored people are laid to rest.

Valhalla appears in the POETIC EDDA (especially in "GRIMNIRSMAL"), in the PROSE EDDA, and as Walhalla in Richard Wagner's THE RING OF THE NIEBELUNG.

See THE HALL OF DEAD HEROES (below) and the VALKYRIES.

The Hall of Dead Heroes VALHALLA, the Hall of Dead Heroes, was built by ODIN, the All-Father, warrior god of the AESIR. Valhalla was situated in GLADSHEIM, Odin's realm in ASGARD. It was splendid indeed, the most beautiful hall there. The roof was tiled with shining shields; the rafters were flashing spears; and on the benches were fine suits of armor, ready for the warriors to put on. It was Odin's plan to receive all the brave men who had died as heroes on earth and give them everlasting life, so that they could help the gods fight the giants at RAGNAROK, the end of the world.

As Odin stood at VALGRIND, the gate of Valhalla, a golden eagle hovered over his head. His two ravens, HUGI and MUNIN (Thought and Memory) sat on his shoulders, and the wolves FREKI (Fierce) and GREKI (Greedy) panted at his side. Beside him stood his two sons, HERMOD and BRAGI. Soon they heard the clatter of horses' hooves on BIFROST, the Rainbow Bridge, and an awesome sight met their eyes.

THESE CARVINGS FROM STONES IN GOTLAND, SWEDEN, SHOW (1) WARRIORS RAISING THEIR DRINKING HORNS AND (2) THE ROASTING OF THE PIG IN VALHALLA.

The VALKYRIES, Odin's splendid warrior maidens (some were his daughters), had put on their gleaming armor and gone down to MIDGARD, or Middle Earth, to choose which warriors were brave enough and strong enough to be rewarded with a new life in Valhalla. Now they returned with the heroes, or EINHERIAR, who had been slain in battle, but were now miraculously alive, their wounds healed, their health robust.

The maidens donned white robes and poured MEAD from drinking horns into the soldiers' goblets, which were the bony skulls of their stricken enemies. The supply of mead was never-ending, for it came from the enchanted she-goat HEIDRUN, who nibbled on the leaves of LAERED, the tree around which the hall was built.

The food was abundant too. It came from another magical creature, the boar SAEHRIMNIR. Each night Saehrimnir was killed, cooked and eaten by the hungry heroes. Each morning the boar would rise up again, ready to go through the whole ritual again. The heroes never went hungry or thirsty, despite their enormous appetites, and Odin looked on with approval.

Odin bade the warriors put on the shining new armor and find the horses in the courtyard. They could fight all day to their hearts' content. If they were wounded, they would be healed. If they were killed, they would come back to life again, ready to enjoy another night of feasting.

And so it was that Odin gradually built up a vast army of the world's best warriors, who would march out of the 540 doors of Valhalla, 800 strong, and valiantly fight beside Odin and the Aesir gods at Ragnarok.

VALI (1) The son of LOKI and SIGYN, and brother of NARVI. After they have captured Loki, the gods turn Vali into a wolf who tears out the entrails of Narvi. The gods use the entrails to bind Loki. (See "Loki's Punishment," under LOKI.)

VALI (2) The youngest son of the god ODIN. His mother was RINDA. Vali avenged Balder's death (see under BALDER) by slaying the blind god HODUR with his arrow. (See "Vali, The Avenger," below.) He was one of the few gods to survive RAGNAROK, the end of the world.

Vali is a personification of the light of lengthening days as spring approaches. Because rays of light were often depicted as arrows, Vali was usually represented and worshiped as an archer. For that reason his month in old Norwegian calendars is designated by the sign of the bow and is called *Lios-beri*, the "light bringer." As *Lios-beri* falls between the modern calendar's mid-January and mid-February, the early Christians dedicated this period to Saint Valentine, who also was a skillful archer and like Vali was said to be the harbinger of brightening days, the awakener of tender springtime sentiments and the patron of lovers.

Vali, The Avenger VALI was the youngest son of the god ODIN. This myth tells of Vali's origins and of how he avenged the death of his half brother, BALDER.

When Balder, Odin's beloved son, began having frightening dreams, Odin made a journey to HEL to seek the knowledge of an ancient sybil. She told Odin that Balder would be killed and that his death would be avenged by another son of Odin's, VALI, as yet unborn. The child's mother would be RINDA. Vali would slay HODUR (Balder's killer) when he was but one night old, with his hands still unwashed and his hair uncombed.

Odin then sent HERMOD, the messenger of the gods, to the wicked but powerful wizard ROSTIOFF, in Lapland, to find out more.

Hermod took Odin's horse, SLEIPNIR, and Odin's runic spear, and set off. The journey was long and there were many perils, but at last Hermod reached the desolate country where the wizard dwelt. Rostioff was not welcoming. He took the form of a terrible giant and approached Hermod with a strong rope. But Hermod struck him with the magic staff and the giant fell at once. Hermod bound Rostioff with his own rope.

The wizard promised to help Hermod if he could be freed from the rope. Hermod loosened the ties. Rostioff chanted spells until the sky grew dark; then the sky reddened into a vision of blood—the blood of Balder. Out of it rose a beautiful woman with a boy-child in her arms. The boy leapt to the ground and immediately started to grow into a man. He shot an arrow into the gloom and then the vision disappeared.

The wizard explained that the woman was Rinda, daughter of King BILLING of the Ruthenians. She was to be the mother of Vali, who would slay Hodur with his bow and arrow.

Hermod took the news back to Odin.

Then Odin disguised himself as an ordinary man and set off to find and win Rinda. He easily won favor with King Billing, but beautiful Rinda was strong-headed and resisted Odin through many of his cleverest disguises. He won her in the end by using magic RUNES, and she agreed to marry him.

Nine months later Vali, newborn child with hands as yet unwashed and hair uncombed, walked over BIFROST into ASGARD. To everyone's amazement he started to grow and grow, until he was as big as a man. Then Odin knew that the boy was his son Vali. Vali drew an arrow from the quiver that he would always carry and shot it at Hodur. Hodur died instantly, and Baldur's death was avenged.

Vali became one of the youngest warrior gods, a god of light, and was one of the few to survive RAGNAROK, the end of the world.

This story is told in the POETIC EDDA, "Balder's Dreams."

VALKYRIES (Choosers of the Slain) Warrior maidens of the god ODIN. They chose men doomed to die in battle and brought them to Odin's VALHALLA (Hall of the Slain). Here the resurrected heroes enjoyed a life of unending feasting and fighting, preparing for RAGNAROK, the end of the world.

The maidens went down to earth (MIDGARD) in full armor, their golden hair flying from underneath their winged helmets. They would hover over the chosen warriors in the thick of battle. When a hero fell, dead or mortally wounded, a Valkyrie would sweep him up and carry him on horseback to ASGARD, where the gods lived.

The Valkyries had such names as Shrieker and Screamer, Storm Raiser, Axe Time, Spear Bearer, Shield Bearer, Mist and others. The number of Valkyries varied between six, nine, and 13 at a time.

In some stories FREYA herself was the goddess-leader of the Valkyries. She was allowed to choose warriors to be entertained in her hall, SESSRUMNIR, in her realm, FOLKVANGER, instead of sending them to Odin's Valhalla.

In Valhalla, the Valkyrie maidens would don graceful gowns and serve the EINHERIAR (slain heroes) with food and drink.

Most of the maidens were from Asgard, daughters of the gods and goddesses. Some were Odin's daughters. Odin allowed some of the maidens to take the form of beautiful white swans. But if a Valkyrie was seen by an earthman without her swanlike disguise, she would become an ordinary mortal and could never again return to Valhalla.

THE VALKYRIES, ODIN'S WARRIOR MAIDENS, CARRIED DEAD HEROES TO VALHALLA.

Richard Wagner wrote an opera *The Valkyries* (*Die Walküre*) as part of THE RING OF THE NIBELUNG cycle. It was first performed in Munich, Austria, in 1870. In it BRUNHILDA is chief of the Valkyries. Wagner's "Ride of the Valkyries" is cited as one of the most stirring pieces of 19th-century orchestral music.

VANAHEIM The realm of the VANIR, gods of fertility, peace and plenty.

VANIR A race of gods and goddesses who lived in VANAHEIM. They were the original gods, more ancient than the AESIR. They were gods of fertility. Chief among them were the twin deities FREY and FREYA. After the war with the Aesir (see THE WAR BETWEEN THE AESIR AND THE VANIR), Frey, Freya and their father, NIORD, went to live in ASGARD, home of the Aesir. After that war, all the gods were referred to as Aesir. The Vanir gods brought peace and plenty to the land. They also brought their knowledge of magic and witchcraft and instructed the Aesir in its practice. The Vanir were worshiped for centuries in northern lands.

VASTY The giant SKRYMIR. Vasty is the name used for the giant in some English retellings of the myth, particularly those intended for young readers.

VE One of ODIN's brothers, along with VILI; son of BOR and the giantess BESTLA. Together the three sons of Bor created the earth and the heavens from the body of the giant YMIR (see CREATION) and "The First Humans" (see CREATION) from the trunks of two trees. It was Ve who gave the humans warmth and color.

In the "VOLUSPA" the three sons of Bor are called Odin, HOENIR (Vili) and Lodur (Ve).

VEGTAM (Wanderer) The name taken by the god ODIN when he went to visit the VALA. He claimed to be the son of Valtam. Odin went to the Vala to seek help for his beloved son BALDER.

VERDANDE (the Present) One of the three NORNS, or Fates. She is usually pictured as looking straight ahead.

VIDAR Son of the god ODIN and the kindly giantess GRID. His home was called VIDI (or Landvidi), a place of tall grasses, wildflowers and growing saplings, a silent and peaceful place. Vidar, too, was known for his silence. But it was he who would avenge his father's death at RAGNAROK, the end of the world. On that day Vidar leapt from his horse and attacked the wolf FENRIS, who had devoured Odin. He placed one foot on the beast's lower jaw and pushed on the upper jaw with his hands, until the monster was torn in two.

Legend has it that Vidar wore a special shoe or boot that had been made by snippings cobblers saved over the years as they trimmed the leather they used for toes and heels of shoes. Another story says that it was GRID who made the shoe for Vidar.

Vidar was one of the few gods who survived

THIS MEDIEVAL ENGRAVING SHOWS A COBBLER MAKING SHOES.

Ragnarok and became one of the rulers of the new world.

A famous stone at Gosforth Church, in Cumbria, England, shows Vidar fighting with Fenris.

VIDFINN   The father of the moon children, BIL and YUKI.

VIDI   The home of the god VIDAR. It was a silent and peaceful place, full of grasses and flowers and saplings. Sometimes called Landvidi.

VIGRID or VIGRITH (Field of Battle)   The immense plain, stretching 120 leagues in every direction, on which the bloody battle of RAGNAROK was fought.

VIKINGS (People of the Inlets)   Scandinavian warriors who raided the coasts and inlets of Europe and the British Isles from the 9th to the 12th centuries ("the Viking Age"). Their greatest achievements were in shipbuilding and navigation (see SHIPS AND SHIP BURIALS). They ventured as far as Greenland, Iceland and North America. The typical LONGSHIP was a graceful vessel with a high prow adorned with the figure of an animal, often a dragon, and a high curved stern. It had a square sail and was powered by oarsmen who hung their shields over the side of the ship. The Vikings founded colonies in Nor-

way, Denmark and Sweden as well as in the British Isles, around the Mediterranean, in Russia and in North America. Their mythological and heroic legends form the content of Old Norse literature.

The Viking Age ended in the 12th century with the coming of Christianity to Scandinavia and the rise of European states, whose people were able to join together and protect themselves against further Viking invasions and raids. Many Vikings settled down in the lands that they had previously raided. They came to be known by the names of the new states — Danes, Norsemen, Swedes, Normans and, in Russia, Varangians.

In spite of their reputation for ferocity, not all Vikings were warriors. Most of them were farmers, hunters and fishermen, leading peaceful lives and having a stable social structure. Family and social bonds were vitally important, for

A VIKING WARRIOR.

many communities were small and isolated, especially in the middle of the dark, grim northern winters. The literature that has come down to us from the Vikings shows that they had a strong streak of humor, common sense and fairness. They were a brave people, acknowledging that life can be hard and that death will come to all, but it is to be met bravely and without complaint. The poem "RIGSTHULA" gives us a detailed picture of how people lived in the Viking Age.

VILI One of ODIN's brothers, along with VE; son of BOR and the giantess BESTLA. Together the three sons of Bor created the earth and the heavens from the body of the giant, YMIR, and "The First Humans" (see under CREATION) from the trunks of two trees. It was Vili who gave the humans their senses and the ability to move.

In the "VOLUSPA" the three sons of Bor are called Odin, HOENIR (Vili) and Lothur (Ve).

VIMUR A rushing river in JOTUNHEIM. The giantess GIALP tried to raise the level of the torrent to drown the god THOR, but Thor hit her with a well-aimed stone and she ran off, howling. (See "Thor and the Giant Geirrod," under THOR.)

THE PROW OF THE VIKING LONGSHIP WAS OFTEN ADORNED WITH THE HEAD OF A DRAGON.

VINGOLF (Friendly Floor) The ASGARD mansion of the goddesses.

VOLSUNGA SAGA A late 13th-century prose epic, telling of the hero SIGURD (called Siegfried in German), youngest son of Volsung. Volsung was a descendant of the god ODIN. The myth "Otter's Ransom" (see under OTTER) and the legends of Sigurd are from the *Volsunga*. Richard Wagner based his operas RING OF THE NIBELUNG in part upon the *Volsunga*.

"VOLUSPA" ("The Sibyl's Prophecy") A Norse poem from Iceland, written in the late 10th or early 11th century. It is perhaps the most important poem in the POETIC EDDA. The poem takes the form of a monologue delivered by the VOLVA, or sibyl, in answer to ODIN's questions. (The question-and-answer format was common in Eddic poems.) The verses deal with the CREATION of the world, of the gods and of human beings; they tell of the first war (see THE WAR BETWEEN THE AESIR AND THE VANIR). They tell of the death of BALDER and of "Loki's Punishment" (see under LOKI). They tell of Loki's monstrous children, FENRIS, the wolf, and JORMUNGAND, the Midgard Serpent, and the part they played at RAGNAROK, the end of the world. At the end of the poem the new world is beginning, a kind of green paradise in GIMLÉ, marred only by the presence of the corpse-eating dragon NITHOG. Many scholars believe that the "Voluspa" is one of the greatest literary achievements in the Germanic world.

VOLVA or VALA A seeress or soothsayer; a kind of magician, usually female, able to see into the future and remember from the past, and capable of giving advice to the living who call her up from the grave for consultations.

In the myth of BALDER, ODIN goes to the underworld to consult a volva or vala to try to find out the reason for his son Balder's frightening dreams. Odin learns from the volva that his son will die.

In the ballad of SVIPDAG, Svipdag calls up the spirit of his mother, GROA, to ask her advice in the wooing of the fair MENGLAD.

The goddess FREYA is associated with the volvas, but no stories survive that describe her role as seeress.

W

WAR BETWEEN THE AESIR AND THE VANIR
The AESIR were the warrior gods who lived in
ASGARD. The VANIR gods existed long before
the first Aesir gods appeared. They were beautiful beings of light and wisdom who lived in
their realm called VANAHEIM, sending forth
gentle sunshine and rain and fertility. They
never set foot in Asgard, nor did they seem to
know of the existence of the Aesir.

But one day, according to some tellings, a
beautiful witch named GULLWEIG or HEID appeared in Asgard, and the seeds were sown for a
battle between the Aesir and the Vanir, the very
first war.

Gullweig had a great hunger for gold. She
could never have enough. She talked about it
constantly, disturbing the gods. Wickedness
had come to Asgard. The great god, ODIN, was
very angry, and decided that the witch must
die.

Three times the Aesir cast Gullweig into the
fire, and three times she rose up, more beautiful
than ever. She went into every hall in Asgard,
casting spells and teaching magic.

Then Gullweig went to the Vanir and told
them how cruelly she had been treated by the
Aesir. Soon an army of Vanir, perhaps led by
brave NIORD, appeared at the walls of Asgard,
ready to avenge Gullweig. Odin cast his spear,
GUNGNIR, and the battle raged until both ar-
mies grew tired of the slaughter. It seemed that
neither side could win—or lose.

And so the leaders of the Aesir and the Vanir
got together to discuss terms. In the end they
agreed that there should be eternal peace between them and that together they would stand
fast against the common enemy, the giants.

To seal the peace treaty, the Aesir and the
Vanir all spat into a jar (as was the custom of the
Northmen when making treaties). From the
spittle was formed KVASIR, the wisest of the
wise. "The Mead of Poetry" (see under ODIN)
tells what happened to Kvasir.

As a sign of good faith, hostages were ex-
changed: Odin sent his brother HOENIR and the
wise god, MIMIR, to live among the Vanir. And
Niord and his son and daughter, FREY and
FREYA, settled in Asgard.

At first the Vanir were delighted with the
handsome Hoenir. They made him one of their
leaders. But they soon noticed that Hoenir
could make no decisions unless he consulted
Mimir. They felt that the Aesir had cheated
them. They didn't dare harm Odin's brother, so
they cut off Mimir's head and sent it back to
Odin. Odin immediately used his magic to re-
store the head to life. He placed it in a spring, to
be known as Mimir's Well, at the foot of the
sacred tree, YGGDRASIL, and he regularly went
to seek its wisdom. (See "Mimir," under
ODIN.)

According to some scholars, this myth may
represent folk memory of the conflict between
the adherents of two different cults, which were
then brought together. After the conflict, the
Aesir win control of the embodiment of wisdom
and inspiration—Kvasir—in one myth and the
head of Mimir in another; they learn the magic
of the Vanir; and all the gods are now referred to
as Aesir.

WATCHMAN OF THE GODS See HEIM-
DALL.

WEDNESDAY The fourth day of the week. It
is named after the god WOTAN, one of the many
names of ODIN. The Romans identified Odin
with their god Mercury. Wednesday is *merco-
ledi* in Italian, *mercredi* in French, and *mier-
coles* in Spanish.

WELL, MIMIR'S See MIMIR.

WELL OF URD See URD.

WELL OF WYRD See URD.

WESTRI (West) One of the four DWARFS who held up the sky (see CREATION).

WHETSTONE A stone used for sharpening tools. The stone is often quartz because of the hardness and sharpness of its broken grains. In Old English *whet* means "to incite or sharpen." In Norse mythology whetstones are made from the pieces of the giant HRUNGNIR's club, which fell apart when it was hit by THOR's hammer. In the story "Thor's Duel with Hrungnir" (see under THOR), some pieces of whetstone lodged in Thor's head, giving him a headache whenever whetstones were carelessly moved or dropped near him.

In the story of how the great god ODIN obtained "The Mead of Poetry" (see under ODIN), Odin uses a whetstone to sharpen the workers' tools. The workers are so eager to have the whetstone that they kill each other with their sharpened weapons in a wild scramble.

An ancient thunder god worshiped by the Lapps was said to have a piece of whetstone, or flint, stuck in his head, along with a piece of iron. If one were struck against the other, fire could be created. And at Sutton Hoo, in England, an impressive whetstone, thought to be a scepter, was found in a 7th-century grave. Clearly, whetstones had properties revered by the ancients.

WYRD See URD.

Y

YDALIR (Yew Dales) The valleys where YEW trees grow. The home of ULL, the winter god of skiers, snowshoes and hunting.

YEW An evergreen tree of the family Taxaceae. In ancient superstitions the European yew (*Taxus baccata*) was thought to have magic properties. It was planted in graveyards to ward off evil spirits and can still be seen today in English graveyards. At YULETIDE its logs were burned in fireplaces to bring good fortune for the coming season, and some say it gave its name to the YULE season. The yew's dark-green leaves and pink berries are poisonous. Its flexible wood made excellent material for hunting bows, which, because of the poison, were thought to be doubly potent in killing. Yew trees can live for many years and are symbols of immortality. In Norse mythology YDALIR (Yew Dales) was the home of the winter god ULL.

YGGDRASIL The ash tree of Norse myth, called the World Tree because it forms a link between all the NINE WORLDS. At the uppermost level are ASGARD (home of the AESIR gods), VANAHEIM, (home of the VANIR gods), and ALFHEIM (home of the light ELVES).

On the next level lie MIDGARD (Earth, the home of humankind); JOTUNHEIM (home of the JOTUNS, or giants); SVARTALFHEIM (home of the dark elves); and NIDAVELLIR (home of the DWARFS). In the dark underworld Yggdrasil's roots reach MUSPELLHEIM (land of fire), and NIFLHEIM, with its stronghold, HEL (land of the dead).

The roots of Yggdrasil are watered by three wells. One is the Well of WYRD or URD, which is a sacred place tended by the three NORNS and where the gods sit in council.

The second is the Well of MIMIR, in which is preserved the head of the wisest of all beings, Mimir. ODIN himself consults Mimir when he is in need of knowledge.

The third spring is VERGELMIR, in Niflheim, the land of the dead. The foul dragon NITHOG lives here, forever nibbling at the roots of Yggdrasil. Writhing serpents breathe clouds of venom onto the roots of Yggdrasil. Huge stags and goats tear leaves and bark from the tree.

But Yggdrasil survives all these torments, helped by the NORNS who sprinkle Urd's water upon the roots. It will survive RAGNAROK, the end of the world, though it will tremble. LIF and LIFTHRASIR will hide in the depths of the tree, fed on its dew and emerge afterward to repeople the earth.

In the topmost branches of Yggdrasil sits a mighty eagle (with a small hawk upon its brow), surveying the world. A squirrel, RATATOSK, scampers up and down the tree bearing tales from Nithog to the eagle and back again.

Once Odin hanged himself from the branches of Yggdrasil for nine nights to learn the secret of the RUNES. (See "Odin: Lord of the Gallows," under ODIN). Norsemen sometimes called the gallows a horse (*drasil*) and Odin *Ygg* (terrible one).

A tree is commonly used in myths to symbolize long life, fertility, regeneration and knowledge. In the Bible, Adam and Eve eat the fruit of the tree of knowledge. The menora, a sevenbranched candlestick, derives from an ancient Mesopotamian tree-of-life symbol. The Christmas tree has its roots in ancient pagan customs, as does the English MAYPOLE.

YMIR (Confused Noise) The first giant, or JOTUN. He was formed from ice and fire at the beginning of time in the vast chasm of GINNUNGAGAP, which lay between icy NIFLHEIM and fiery MUSPELLHEIM. Ymir was nourished by the first cow, AUDHUMLA, and he grew to a huge size.

As Ymir slept, male and female giants sprang from his armpits, and from his feet grew a sixheaded troll. From these creatures began the race of frost giants, all huge and hideously ugly.

After the first gods, ODIN, VILI and VE, were born from the giants BOR and BESTLA, the gods quarreled constantly with the giants, and at last killed Ymir.

From his body the gods created MIDGARD, the Middle Earth. Ymir's blood formed the seas and all the lakes and rivers. His flesh became the hills and plains, his bones the mountains and his teeth the rocks. His hair formed trees and all vegetation.

The gods placed Ymir's skull as a dome over the earth, and his brains were cast to the winds to become clouds.

See CREATION.

YOUNGER EDDA   Also known as the PROSE EDDA, written by SNORRI STURLUSON.

YUKI   See BIL AND YUKI.

YULE, YULETIDE   The time of year that many people now call Christmastime. The word possibly comes from the old English word *yole* (which in turn comes from Icelandic *jol*), meaning "to cry aloud or yell." It seems likely that people would indeed shout for joy when they discovered that the days were getting longer at the time of the winter solstice (around December 22). Many pagan customs survive to this day to celebrate Yule, including the burning of the YULE LOG and feasting on a BOAR's head (or at least its modern equivalent of roast pork or ham).

YULE LOG   The log, or chunk of wood (often from the YEW tree), burned at Yuletide in many northern countries. Traditionally, a piece of wood from the fire must be saved to start the next year's fire. The custom originated in ancient times, when lighting a fire was a form of rejoicing (in this case, for the lengthening of the daylight hours that begins around December 22 in northern climes). (See YULE.)

SELECTED BIBLIOGRAPHY

GENERAL BOOKS ON MYTHOLOGY

Barber, Richard. *A Companion to World Mythology.* New York: Delacorte Press, 1979.

Bulfinch, Thomas. *Bulfinch's Mythology.* New York: Crowell, 1970.

Brewer, Ebenezer. *Brewer's Dictionary of Phrase and Fable.* Revised by Ivor H. Evans. New York: Harper & Row, 1981.

Campbell, Joseph. *The Hero With a Thousand Faces.* New York: Pantheon Books, 1949; paperback, Bollingen Series, Princeton, N.J.: Princeton Press, 1968.

———. *The Power of Myth,* with Bill Moyers. New York: Doubleday, 1988.

Cotterell, Arthur. *A Dictionary of World Mythology.* O.U.P., 1979, 1986.

Eliot, Alexander, ed. *Myths.* New York: McGraw-Hill, 1976.

Frazer, James G. *The Golden Bough.* London: Macmillan, 1912; abridged edition, 1922; paperback, 1957.

Gaster, Theodore H., ed. *The New Golden Bough: A New Abridgement of the Classic Work by Sir James George Frazer.* New York: Criterion Books, 1959.

Mercatante, Anthony S. *Facts On File Encyclopedia of World Mythology and Legend.* New York: Facts On File, 1988.

New Larousse Encyclopedia of Mythology. Translated by Richard Aldington and Delano Ames. London and New York: Hamlyn, 1968.

BOOKS ON NORSE MYTHOLOGY

Branston, Brian. *Gods of the North.* New York: Thames & Hudson, 1955, 1980.

———. *Gods and Heroes from Viking Mythology.* New York: Schocken Books, 1982.

Crossley-Holland, Kevin. *The Norse Myths.* New York: Pantheon Books, 1980.

———. *Axe-Age, Wolf-Age.* London: Andre Deutsch Limited, 1985.

D'Aulaire, Ingri and Parin. *Norse Gods and Giants.* New York: Doubleday, 1986.

Davidson, H. R. Ellis. *Gods and Myths of Northern Europe.* London: Penguin Books, 1964.

———. *Scandinavian Mythology.* London: Hamlyn, 1982; New York: Peter Bedricks Books, 1986.

Green, Roger Lancelyn. *Myths of the Norsemen.* Puffin, 1982.

Grimm Brothers. *Teutonic Mythology.* London: George Bell and Sons, 1883. Reissued New York: Dover Publications, 1966.

Guerber, H. A. *Myths of the Norsemen.* London: George G. Harrap & Co., 1908.

Snorri Sturluson. *The Prose Edda: Tales from Norse Mythology.* Translated by Jean I. Young. Berkeley: University of California, 1964, 1971.

Strayer, Joseph Reese, ed. *Dictionary of the Middle Ages.* New York: Scribner, 1989.

Turville-Petre, E. O. G. *Myth and Religion of the North.* London: Weidenfeld and Nicholson, 1964.

INDEX

Note: Boldface numbers indicate main headings;
italic numbers indicate illustrations

105